From ordinary to extraordinary

Becoming a Corporate Athlete

By
Linda Patel

Copyright 2024 Linda Patel. All rights reserved.

No part of this book may be reproduced in any form or by any electronic or mechanical means, including information storage and retrieval systems, without permission in writing from the author. The only exception is a reviewer who may quote brief excerpts in a review.

Although the author and publisher have made every effort to ensure that the information in this book was correct at press time, the author and publisher do not assume and hereby disclaim any liability to any party for any loss, damage, or disruption caused by errors or omissions, whether such errors or omissions result from negligence, accident, or any other cause.

This publication is designed to provide accurate and authoritative information with regard to the subject matter covered. It is sold with the understanding that the publisher is not engaged in rendering professional services. If legal advice or other expert assistance is required, the services of a competent professional should be sought.

The fact that an organization or website is referred to in this work as a citation and/or a potential source of further information does not mean that the author or the publisher endorses the information the organization or website may provide or recommendations it may make.

Please remember that Internet websites listed in this work may have changed or disappeared between when this work was written and when it is read.

About the Author

Linda Patel, the author of this book, is a seasoned executive with over 25 years of experience in various leadership roles at a premier wealth management firm. As a Managing Director, Linda has consistently demonstrated exceptional strategic vision and a keen ability to navigate the complexities of the financial industry. Her extensive expertise in leading diverse teams and driving organizational success has earned her a reputation as a dynamic and influential leader. Throughout her career, Linda has been a steadfast advocate for continuous learning and professional growth, inspiring countless individuals to achieve their full potential in the corporate world.

Acknowledgments

Writing this book has been an incredible journey, and I am deeply grateful to the many people who supported and inspired me along the way. First and foremost, I want to express my heartfelt thanks to my husband, Rock, and our son, Jake. Your unwavering support, encouragement, and patience have been my anchor throughout this process. Rock, your belief in me gave me the courage to pursue this dream, and Jake, your boundless enthusiasm and curiosity remind me every day of the importance of perseverance and passion. I am also profoundly grateful to my former colleague, mentor, and friend, Larry Kloth. Larry, your wisdom, guidance, and friendship have been invaluable to me. You inspired me to finally take the leap and write this book, and for that, I will always be thankful. Your influence is woven throughout these pages, and I hope this book reflects the lessons and insights you have shared with me over the years. To all my colleagues, past and present, thank you for the shared experiences and knowledge that have shaped my professional journey. Your collaboration and support have been instrumental in my growth as a leader. Lastly, I want to thank my family and friends who have cheered me on, offered feedback, and provided much-needed encouragement. Your love and support have been my strength, and I am deeply grateful for each of you. This book would not have been possible without the collective support and inspiration from all of you. Thank you for believing in me and for being a part of this journey.

Contents

About the Author iii
Acknowledgments iv
Contents v
Introduction 1
Chapter 1: Understanding the Corporate Athlete 5
    Defining the Corporate Athlete 5
    The Importance of Physical, Mental, and Emotional Balance 8
Chapter 2: Physical Conditioning for Optimal Performance 11
    Importance of Physical Fitness 11
    Developing a Sustainable Exercise Routine 14
Chapter 3: Mental Conditioning and Resilience 18
    Building Mental Toughness 18
    Strategies for Stress Management and Focus 22
Chapter 4: Emotional Intelligence in the Corporate Arena 26
    Understanding and Managing Emotions 26
    Building Strong Relationships and Effective Communication 30
Chapter 5: Time Management and Productivity 34
    Prioritizing Tasks and Setting Goals 34
    Techniques for Maximizing Efficiency 36
Chapter 6: Leadership and Team Dynamics 41
    Traits of Effective Leaders 41

    Building and Leading High-Performance Teams 44

Chapter 7: Continuous Learning and Adaptability 48
    The Importance of Lifelong Learning 48
    Adapting to Change in the Corporate World 52

Chapter 8: Crafting Your Personal Brand 56
    Identifying Your Unique Value Proposition 56
    Gathering Feedback to Understand How Others Perceive You 59
    Creating a Compelling Personal Narrative 61
    Enhancing Your Online Presence 63
    Leveraging Public Speaking and Writing 66

Chapter 9: Taking Action 70
    Case Studies and Examples 70
    Actionable Tips and Exercises 73
    1. Daily Physical Fitness Routine 74
    2. Mental Toughness Drills 74
    3. Emotional Intelligence Enhancements 75
    4. Time Management Techniques 75
    5. Leadership Skill Development 76
    6. Continuous Learning and Adaptability 76
    7. Personal Branding Activities 77
    8. Creating a Personal Action Plan 77
    Interviews and Expert Insights: 78

Conclusion 82

Appendix A: Appendix 85
    Additional Resources 85
    Recommended Readings 86
    Additional Resources 87
    Recommended Readings 89

Introduction

Welcome to a journey that is less about the destination and more about the transformative experience that will shape you into a successful corporate executive. If you're here, it's likely because you aspire to reach new heights, break through invisible barriers, and excel in the demanding yet rewarding world of corporate leadership. The goal of this book is to equip you with the tools and insights you need to thrive, not just survive, in the corporate world. Adaptability, resilience, and strategic thinking are more important than ever, and mastering these skills can set you apart from the crowd.

Embarking on this path, you may already realize that the corporate arena is akin to an elite athletic competition. Just as professional athletes train rigorously to perform at their peak, successful corporate executives must condition their minds and bodies to withstand the pressures and demands of the business world. The parallels between the two are striking: both require discipline, mental acuity, emotional intelligence, and a relentless focus on continuous improvement.

So, what does it take to become a "corporate athlete"? It's more than just a catchy phrase; it's a holistic approach to personal and professional development. In the pages that follow, you'll learn how to foster physical fitness, cultivate mental resilience, hone emotional intelligence, and optimize your time and productivity. Together, these elements create a foundation that will support your ambitions and guide you through the complexities of corporate life.

Let's start by understanding that success in the corporate realm doesn't materialize overnight. It's a cumulative process, built on daily habits and decisions. The journey involves challenging your own limits, stepping out of your comfort zone, and being prepared to think and act strategically. And while the road may often be steep, each step taken is a testament to your dedication and potential.

Balance is crucial. In a world that glorifies hustle and endless work hours, it's easy to overlook the importance of a balanced life. Physical health, mental clarity, and emotional well-being are not peripheral considerations; they are fundamental pillars that support sustainable success. This book delves deep into each of these facets, providing actionable insights and strategies to help you find and maintain that equilibrium.

We'll begin with the basics of physical conditioning. After all, a strong body fosters a strong mind. You'll discover the significance of physical fitness in maintaining energy levels, reducing stress, and enhancing cognitive function. We'll guide you through developing a sustainable exercise routine that suits your lifestyle, one that you can stick to in the long haul.

Next, we'll venture into the realm of mental conditioning and resilience. The corporate world is fraught with challenges that require sharp mental acuity and a resilient mindset. We'll explore techniques to build mental toughness, manage stress effectively, and retain focus amidst distractions. Mental conditioning is not just about overcoming adversity but thriving on it.

Our journey would be incomplete without delving into emotional intelligence. Strong interpersonal skills and emotional awareness can significantly impact your professional relationships and communication effectiveness. You'll learn how to understand and manage your own emotions, as well as build strong, symbiotic relationships with those around you.

From ordinary to extraordinary

Time management and productivity are the cornerstones of a successful career. Prioritizing tasks, setting realistic goals, and maximizing efficiency are skills that every corporate athlete must master. We'll share practical techniques that can help you make the most of your time, ensuring that your efforts are both effective and impactful.

The role of a leader is multifaceted and crucial in shaping an organization's success. We'll explore the traits that define effective leaders and provide insights into building and leading high-performance teams. Leadership isn't just about commanding; it's about inspiring and mobilizing teams towards shared goals.

In today's fast-paced corporate landscape, staying a step ahead means embracing continuous learning and adaptability. The willingness to learn and adapt is what distinguishes successful executives from the rest. We'll emphasize the significance of lifelong learning and offer strategies to help you stay agile and responsive to change.

Consider this book as your playbook for corporate excellence. Each chapter builds on the previous ones, collectively offering a comprehensive guide to conditioning your mind and body for the challenges and opportunities that lie ahead. Our aim is not just to impart knowledge but to inspire action, fostering a mindset that embraces growth and resilience.

As we embark on this exploration together, remember that the principles you'll discover are meant to be applied and experienced. Reading alone won't bring about transformation; it's the application of these insights in your daily life that will truly make the difference. Prepare to engage actively with the concepts, practice diligently, and reflect on your progress.

Let this be the start of a transformative journey where you rise to your full potential, harnessing both inner and outer resources to excel in the corporate world. Success isn't a matter of chance; it's a matter of choice and preparation. Welcome to a new chapter of growth and achievement. Let's begin.

Chapter 1:
Understanding the Corporate Athlete

In the fast-paced world of corporate athletics, where boardrooms replace stadiums and strategy documents serve as game plans, the term "Corporate Athlete" encapsulates a holistic approach to thriving in a high-stakes environment. This chapter serves as a gateway to understanding how executives can sharpen their skills and elevate their performance by achieving a harmonious balance between physical health, mental resilience, and emotional intelligence. Imagine the synergy of an athlete's discipline, a monk's mindfulness, and a leader's vision all fused into one persona. Successful corporate athletes recognize that true excellence isn't confined to isolated prowess but lies in the seamless integration of body, mind, and spirit. By mastering this triad, they don't just reach their peaks—they redefine them, pushing the boundaries of what's possible in the corporate arena.

Defining the Corporate Athlete

When we think of athletes, names like Michael Jordan or Serena Williams may leap to mind—those titans of sport who push their physical and mental limits to excel at the highest levels. Yet, in the corridors of corporate offices, another type of athlete thrives, often less visible but equally dedicated and driven. This is the corporate athlete. What defines a corporate athlete, and how does one transition from merely being a part of the workforce to becoming this elite performer?

A corporate athlete is someone who approaches their corporate career with the same intensity, discipline, and strategic mindset as a professional sports athlete. They understand that success in the corporate world demands more than just intellectual acumen; it requires a well-rounded approach to physical fitness, mental resilience, and emotional balance. In the high-stakes environment of corporate life, these individuals strive to excel by harnessing and honing their capabilities across these three dimensions.

One distinguishing feature of a corporate athlete is their relentless pursuit of excellence. They are not content with mediocrity or settling for the status quo. Like any elite athlete, they are driven by goals and objectives, continuously setting higher benchmarks for themselves. They see their career not as a series of isolated tasks but as a cohesive and dynamic journey, where each day presents an opportunity for growth and improvement.

The physical aspect cannot be understated. The modern corporate environment demands long hours, often in sedentary positions, which can lead to fatigue and burnout if not managed correctly. A corporate athlete understands that maintaining physical fitness is paramount. Regular exercise is not just a health choice; it becomes a strategic tool for maintaining high energy levels, sharp focus, and extended endurance. They incorporate a disciplined exercise regimen, understanding that a healthy body supports a sharp and resilient mind.

Mental toughness is another cornerstone of the corporate athlete's profile. High-pressure situations, tight deadlines, and the need for agile decision-making are par for the course in the corporate world. A corporate athlete develops strategies to enhance mental endurance and resilience. This includes practices such as mindfulness, visualization, and continuous learning to stay at the top of their game. They approach challenges as opportunities, maintaining a positive mindset that fuels their drive and innovation.

Moreover, emotional intelligence (EI) is crucial. The corporate athlete excels in understanding and managing not just their emotions but also those of their colleagues and subordinates. Effective communication, empathy, and the ability to build strong, trusting relationships are integral. While physical and mental conditioning are often visible through performance metrics and outputs, emotional intelligence reflects in the seamless collaboration and cohesive team dynamics that a corporate athlete fosters.

What distinguishes a corporate athlete from their peers is the holistic and integrated approach they take towards their professional and personal development. They understand that these elements are intertwined, and neglecting one can affect the other domains. Therefore, they are proactive in seeking balance and synergy among these aspects, ensuring that none are left to chance.

Balancing these components consistently is no small feat. It requires a disciplined, structured approach and a willingness to continually adapt and evolve. This involves setting clear, achievable goals that encompass the physical, mental, and emotional dimensions of their lives. By setting these goals, they develop a roadmap that guides their actions and decisions, ensuring alignment with their broader vision of success.

In essence, the corporate athlete epitomizes an individual who is deeply invested in their own growth, both professionally and personally. They understand that the road to success is paved with continuous effort, strategic planning, and a commitment to maintain and enhance their overall well-being. They embrace challenges with a competitive spirit, leveraging them as opportunities to grow stronger and more adept.

Ultimately, defining the corporate athlete leads us to appreciate the multifaceted nature of success in the corporate realm. It's not merely about climbing the corporate ladder or achieving financial success; it's about cultivating a lifestyle of excellence that permeates every facet of one's life. The corporate athlete views their career as an arena where they continually test their limits, improve their skills, and achieve peak performance.

The Importance of Physical, Mental, and Emotional Balance

Understanding the corporate athlete is not just about achieving business successes through sheer determination and work ethic. It's about adopting a comprehensive approach that involves balancing your physical, mental, and emotional spheres. This balance isn't merely advantageous; it's crucial for longevity and sustainability in a high-pressure corporate environment.

Physical fitness is often the first domain neglected by busy professionals, but it should be the foundation upon which other aspects of corporate excellence are built. Regular exercise not only enhances physical health but also significantly boosts cognitive function and emotional well-being. The endorphins released during physical activity play a pivotal role in stress reduction, making it easier to tackle demanding corporate challenges with a clearer mind.

Imagine navigating through a sea of emails, meetings, and deadlines without physical vitality. It's almost impossible. A well-conditioned body leads to greater stamina and resilience, allowing corporate athletes to be more productive and engaged in their work. Moreover, it prevents the muscle soreness, fatigue, and lethargy that can severely hamper productivity. Physical fitness facilitates superior performance by promoting a healthier body-mind connection.

While physical conditioning lays the groundwork, mental conditioning ensures that the corporate athlete remains sharp, focused, and resolute. Building mental toughness involves cultivating a mindset that embraces challenges, demonstrates patience, and continually seeks growth. This mental resilience is what separates those who merely survive in the corporate world from those who truly thrive.

Strategic mental training could involve practice in mindfulness, meditation, or cognitive behavioral techniques aimed at fostering a better understanding of one's mental processes. Such practices help in managing stress, focusing attention, and maintaining a positive outlook amidst setbacks. Corporate athletes who invest in their mental health are better equipped to handle the pressures of high-stakes decision-making and complex problem-solving.

The emotional dimension is equally vital but often overlooked. Emotional intelligence is not just about understanding and managing your own emotions; it's also about navigating the emotions of others. In the corporate world, where teamwork and interpersonal communication are key, this ability can significantly impact one's leadership effectiveness and the overall team dynamic.

Developing emotional intelligence involves self-awareness, self-regulation, empathy, social skills, and intrinsic motivation. Those who master these skills can build stronger relationships, communicate more effectively, and foster a positive work environment. Emotional balance enables the corporate athlete to navigate difficult interactions and conflict situations with grace and professionalism, turning potential points of contention into opportunities for collaboration and growth.

The interplay between these three dimensions – physical, mental, and emotional – creates a synergistic effect. A strong body supports a resilient mind, which in turn helps manage emotions more effectively. Conversely, emotional well-being can improve mental clarity and focus, which can inspire greater physical activity and fitness. It's a virtuous cycle that needs continuous nurturing and attention.

A balanced approach isn't a one-time fix but a lifelong commitment. Corporate athletes must constantly evaluate and adjust their physical, mental, and emotional practices. It's essential to integrate habits that support all three dimensions into daily routines. For instance, pairing regular exercise with mental relaxation techniques and emotional check-ins can go a long way in maintaining holistic balance.

The journey to achieving this balance is personal and varies for each individual. What works for one person may not work for another. Therefore, corporate athletes must stay attuned to their unique needs and preferences, regularly reassessing their routines and making adjustments as necessary. This individualized approach ensures that the balance is not just achieved but also sustained over time.

Moreover, organizations are increasingly recognizing the importance of supporting their employees' well-being across these three dimensions. Providing resources such as gym memberships, mental health days, and emotional intelligence training can significantly enhance employee performance and job satisfaction. Corporate athletes who have the backing of their organizations in these areas are more likely to succeed and lead by example.

Ultimately, the importance of physical, mental, and emotional balance cannot be overstated. It's not just about being good at your job; it's about cultivating a lifestyle that promotes overall well-being and sustained excellence. For anyone looking to excel in the corporate world, this triad of balance forms the bedrock of true success. This commitment to holistic development will ensure that you're not just surviving the corporate hustle but mastering it with poise, vitality, and grace.

Chapter 2: Physical Conditioning for Optimal Performance

Just as a finely tuned engine powers a high-performance car, physical conditioning is the bedrock of a successful corporate executive. Keeping fit is more than just looking good; it's about longevity, energy, and resilience in a demanding professional landscape. Balancing work with a sustainable exercise routine not only enhances your stamina but sharpens your mental acuity, enabling you to tackle daily challenges head-on. Physical fitness leads to higher productivity and mood stabilization, creating a harmonious blend of vigor and focus. By prioritizing physical conditioning, you're not merely preparing for the boardroom but for a long, vibrant career where you're always at your peak. The fusion of discipline in physical fitness with executive responsibilities forms a powerful foundation for optimal performance.

Importance of Physical Fitness

Imagine a finely tuned, high-performance machine. Every cog and gear moves in seamless harmony, pushing the boundaries of efficiency and productivity. This analogy aligns perfectly with the role of physical fitness in the life of a corporate athlete. Physical fitness is not just a complementary aspect of an executive's regimen; it is an integral component that can significantly influence one's professional prowess.

Physical fitness serves as the bedrock upon which other forms of conditioning are built. It is impossible to overstate its importance. A strong, healthy body provides the stamina required to endure long hours, manage stress, and maintain a high level of focus and energy. When you commit to physical fitness, you're essentially investing in the machine that drives your corporate successes.

Indeed, the corporate environment is often likened to a battlefield. In this competitive arena, only the fittest—both mentally and physically—thrive. Being physically fit is not just about looking good; it's about feeling good, too. The mental clarity and emotional stability that come from an active lifestyle are indispensable in navigating the complexities and pressures of the corporate world.

In conversations with top executives, a common thread often emerges: the acknowledgment of physical fitness as a core element of their success. Examples abound of CEOs rising before dawn for their morning runs or hitting the gym before starting their demanding days. These habits aren't coincidental; they are deliberate choices to enhance physical well-being, which in turn, bolsters professional performance.

Consider cardiovascular health, for instance. Regular cardiovascular exercise, such as running, swimming, or cycling, strengthens your heart and lungs. This not only improves your overall health but also boosts your energy levels. With a well-oiled cardiovascular system, you're less likely to experience midday slumps and more capable of sustaining high levels of productivity throughout the day.

Moreover, the role of muscular strength shouldn't be overlooked. Strength-training exercises fortify your muscles, helping you to maintain proper posture and reduce the risk of injuries. This is particularly important for those whose days are spent in front of computers or in boardrooms. Strong muscles support a healthy body structure, enabling you to better handle the physical demands of daily life, both inside and outside the office.

Then there's the undeniable impact of physical fitness on mental health. Engaging in regular physical activity stimulates the production of endorphins, the body's natural mood elevators. These biochemical substances can significantly reduce feelings of stress and anxiety, common companions in the high-stakes corporate world. A regular exercise routine offers not only physical rewards but also emotional resilience.

Let's delve into flexibility and its importance. While strength and cardiovascular health are crucial, flexibility ensures that your body remains limber and agile. Practices like yoga or Pilates can be beneficial for maintaining a full range of motion in your joints. Flexibility training reduces the risk of injuries and helps to manage the physical strain that comes with prolonged periods of sitting or repetitive movements.

Proper nutrition is another cornerstone of physical fitness. The food you consume can either fuel or deplete your energy stores. Adopting a balanced diet rich in essential nutrients ensures that your body gets the vitamins and minerals it needs to function optimally. When your body is well-nourished, your brain is too, leading to enhanced cognitive functions such as memory, focus, and creativity.

Hydration is a critical, yet often overlooked, aspect of physical fitness. The human body is composed largely of water, and maintaining proper hydration levels is essential for all bodily functions. Dehydration can lead to fatigue, lack of concentration, and even more serious health issues. By staying hydrated, you maintain your body's efficiency, which translates to higher productivity and improved mood.

Sleep, often sacrificed in the pursuit of success, is deeply intertwined with physical fitness. Quality sleep is not just about resting; it's when your body undergoes essential repair and maintenance. Consistent physical activity can improve sleep patterns, making it easier to fall asleep and enjoy deeper, more restorative sleep. This, in turn, enhances your alertness and ability to make critical decisions.

It's also worth mentioning the social benefits associated with physical fitness. Participating in team sports or group fitness classes can foster camaraderie and teamwork skills. These are directly transferable to the workplace, where cooperation and collaboration are key. Engaging in physical activities with colleagues can strengthen professional relationships and create a more cohesive work environment.

Finally, the discipline required to maintain physical fitness often spills over into other areas of life. The commitment to a regular exercise regimen necessitates discipline, time management, and perseverance—traits that are incredibly advantageous in a corporate setting. Executives who prioritize physical fitness are often seen as more disciplined, reliable, and motivated, qualities that are highly valued in any professional arena.

In conclusion, the importance of physical fitness in the realm of corporate achievement cannot be overstated. It is a multifaceted tool that enhances not just your physical capabilities, but also your mental agility and emotional resilience. In the pursuit of excellence, investing in your physical fitness is one of the most prudent decisions you can make. The dividends are tangible and significant, propelling you towards peak performance in a demanding corporate landscape.

Developing a Sustainable Exercise Routine

Creating a sustainable exercise routine is the backbone of any successful physical conditioning program, especially for corporate executives who lead demanding lives. The hustle and bustle of corporate life often leave little room for consistent physical activity, making it crucial to develop a balanced, adaptable, and enjoyable exercise regimen.

A sustainable exercise routine starts with understanding your current fitness level and setting realistic goals. It's essential to acknowledge where you are to map out where you want to go. For executives, this means considering both professional obligations and personal health needs. The key to making exercise a regular part of your life is not to see it as an added burden but rather as an integral component of your daily routine. By framing exercise as a non-negotiable meeting with yourself, you create a mindset that prioritizes health.

Begin with small, manageable changes. If you're new to regular exercise, there's no need to start with grueling hour-long sessions at the gym. Instead, incorporate short bouts of activity into your day. A 10-minute walk during lunch or a quick set of push-ups and squats in the morning can make a significant difference over time. The consistency of these small actions builds the foundation for more intense activities later on.

Variety is another critical factor in maintaining a sustainable routine. Engaging in different types of activities not only keeps exercise interesting but also ensures a balanced approach to physical fitness. Incorporate a mix of cardiovascular exercises, strength training, and flexibility work. This could mean alternating between running, lifting weights, and practicing yoga or pilates.

Maintaining motivation over the long term requires finding activities you genuinely enjoy. It's easier to stick to an exercise routine when you're looking forward to the workout rather than dreading it. Experiment with different forms of physical activity to discover what you like best. Whether it's dancing, cycling, hiking, or joining a recreational sports league, there's something out there for everyone.

Setting specific, measurable, and time-bound goals is essential. Rather than vague aspirations like "get fit," aim for concrete milestones. Examples include "complete a 5K run in three months" or "attend a yoga class twice a week." These goals provide clear targets and a sense of accomplishment as you achieve them. Also, tracking your progress helps maintain momentum and allows you to adjust your routine as needed.

A common challenge for many corporate executives is the unpredictable nature of their schedules. Travel, late meetings, and deadlines can disrupt even the best-laid plans. Flexibility in your exercise routine is crucial. When a long day at the office delays your workout plans, have a backup option. Online workout programs, quick in-office exercise sessions, or brief, high-intensity interval training (HIIT) workouts can fit into even the busiest schedules.

Involve others in your fitness journey whenever possible. Finding a workout buddy or joining a fitness class can significantly enhance your commitment and enjoyment. Socializing through exercise adds an element of accountability and makes the experience more enjoyable. Walking meetings, group fitness classes, or team sports can foster connections and encourage a healthy work-life balance.

An often-overlooked component of a sustainable exercise routine is adequate recovery. Rest days and proper sleep are as critical as the workouts themselves. Your body needs time to repair and strengthen itself between workouts. Overtraining can lead to burnout and injuries, making it harder to maintain consistency. Listen to your body and incorporate rest days strategically into your schedule.

Nutrition also plays an essential role in sustaining an exercise routine. Fueling your body with the right nutrients supports performance and recovery. A balanced diet rich in whole foods, lean proteins, healthy fats, and complex carbohydrates will provide the energy needed for workouts and overall health. Avoid fad diets or extreme restrictions that can deplete energy and make you less inclined to exercise.

Technology can be a valuable ally in developing and maintaining a sustainable exercise routine. Fitness apps, wearable trackers, and online communities offer a range of tools for monitoring progress, setting goals, and staying motivated. Many apps provide customizable workout plans that can adapt to your fitness level and schedule, helping you stay on track even when life gets hectic.

Finally, regular reflection on your exercise routine helps ensure it evolves with your changing needs and goals. Periodically reassess your progress, celebrate your successes, and identify areas for improvement. This mindfulness approach not only keeps you on track but also reinforces the habit of making physical fitness a priority in your life.

Incorporating exercise into the demanding life of a corporate executive may seem daunting, yet it's entirely feasible. By focusing on sustainability, enjoying the process, and remaining adaptable, you can build a routine that not only fits your lifestyle but enhances your professional performance and personal well-being.

In essence, developing a sustainable exercise routine is about creating a balanced, enjoyable, and adaptable approach to physical fitness. It's about making exercise not just a task, but a lifestyle choice that propels you toward optimal performance in all areas of life.

The strategies outlined here aim to empower you to prioritize physical conditioning alongside your professional ambitions, crafting a harmonious blend that leads to success both inside and outside the boardroom.

Chapter 3:
Mental Conditioning and Resilience

As we delve deeper into the realm of mental conditioning and resilience, it becomes clear that the corporate landscape demands not just skill, but unwavering mental fortitude. The path of a successful executive is laden with challenges, each one a test of resilience and the ability to thrive under pressure. Developing mental toughness is akin to forging steel; it requires deliberate practice and a clear focus on managing stress and fostering an unwavering mindset. Executives must cultivate strategies to not only handle stress but to transform it into a powerful force that propels them forward. By sharpening their mental resilience, they can navigate uncertainties with confidence and clarity, ensuring consistent peak performance. This chapter uncovers the tools and techniques necessary to master this essential aspect of corporate success, paving the way for sustained excellence and a legacy of leadership.

Building Mental Toughness

In the fast-paced corporate world, challenges and setbacks are inevitable. Building mental toughness, therefore, becomes a cornerstone for not just surviving but thriving in this competitive environment. Mental toughness is essentially the mental or psychological strength that allows individuals to navigate through difficult circumstances, recover from failures, and keep pushing forward despite any hindrances. This section delves into the essence of mental toughness and provides actionable insights on how to cultivate this vital attribute.

Many often mistake mental toughness for the sheer ability to endure pain or stress. While endurance is part of the equation, it's far from the whole picture. Mental toughness includes maintaining focus amid distractions, staying positive when outcomes turn sour, and making quick, effective decisions under pressure. It's about resilience—not just holding up against adversity but bouncing back stronger each time you're knocked down.

Mental toughness is not an innate trait; rather, it is developed through consistent effort and a multitude of experiences. Much like training muscles in the gym, the mind can be conditioned and strengthened over time. Understanding this, it's crucial to look at mental conditioning as a continuous, lifelong endeavor. It's about forging a mindset that remains unyielding even when legitimacy feels debatable, and motivation wanes.

One key aspect of building mental toughness is maintaining a clear and unwavering focus on goals. A corporate executive often faces a barrage of distractions, be it in the form of emails, meetings, or unexpected crises. Learning to prioritize tasks, filtering out noise, and keeping the end goal in sight sharpens one's mental fortitude. This requires not just discipline but also the ability to be adaptable without losing sight of the larger picture.

Visualization is a powerful tool in this arsenal. By mentally rehearsing successful outcomes and positive scenarios, you create a mental blueprint that can be followed during real-life situations. Visualization helps in fostering a sense of familiarity with success, reducing the mental fatigue associated with uncertainty. Professional athletes often use this technique to prepare for games, and corporate athletes can similarly benefit from it.

Building mental toughness also requires embracing failure as an integral part of the growth process. Failures and mistakes are not deterrents but stepping stones. They're invaluable learning opportunities that provide real-world feedback, essential for continuous improvement. The trick is not to internalize failures but to assess them objectively, extract the lessons learned, and move on with renewed vigor.

The role of self-belief and confidence cannot be overstated. A mentally tough executive has an unshakeable belief in their capabilities. This confidence isn't born from arrogance but from a deep understanding of one's strengths and weaknesses. Strengthening this belief requires setting small, achievable milestones that gradually build up one's confidence. As you keep hitting these targets, your self-assurance will grow, fortifying your mental toughness along the way.

Consider the power of a strong support system—both professional and personal. Mentors, colleagues, family, and friends can serve as invaluable sounding boards and sources of encouragement. Sharing experiences and receiving honest feedback help in maintaining a balanced perspective. Surrounding yourself with positive influences can significantly enhance your mental resilience.

Another essential ingredient is stress management. High-pressure environments are a given in the corporate world, and managing this stress is critical for maintaining mental toughness. Techniques like deep breathing, meditation, and mindfulness practices can help you stay calm and grounded. Regular exercise and a balanced diet also play a significant role in stress management; they not only improve physical health but also boost mental clarity.

Developing a routine that blends work, rest, and play ensures that you are neither burned out nor disengaged. Taking regular breaks and vacations to recharge and disconnect from work-related stress is necessary for long-term sustainability. It's essential to recognize the signs of burnout early and take proactive steps to address them.

It's also useful to adopt a learning mindset. Embrace curiosity and adaptability. Staying open to new experiences, soliciting feedback, and continually seeking to improve one's skills and knowledge can significantly contribute to mental toughness. The more adept you are at navigating change and unpredictability, the stronger your mental fortitude will become.

Positive self-talk is another technique for building mental toughness. The way you speak to yourself in your mind impacts your performance more than you might realize. Phrases like "I can handle this" or "I am prepared for what comes next" help in framing challenges positively. This inward encouragement creates a resilient mindset that can withstand adversities.

Emotion regulation is another critical component. As you climb the corporate ladder, the ability to keep your emotions in check becomes increasingly important. High emotional intelligence allows one to navigate complex interpersonal dynamics, making decisions that are not clouded by transient emotions. Being in control of your emotional responses helps in maintaining a composed and unflappable demeanor.

Lastly, keeping a journal can offer surprising benefits. Regularly documenting your thoughts, experiences, and emotional states provides insights into your patterns of behavior and thinking. Journaling can serve as a tool for reflection, allowing you to identify areas where you need to build more mental toughness and track your growth over time.

In conclusion, building mental toughness is a multifaceted endeavor, requiring consistent effort, a positive mindset, and practical strategies. It's about creating a mental landscape where challenges are viewed as opportunities and failures as lessons. Through a blend of visualization, stress management, self-belief, and continuous learning, you can develop the mental resilience needed to excel in the demanding world of corporate leadership.

Strategies for Stress Management and Focus

Stress and focus are the yin and yang of the corporate world, interconnected and interdependent. One cannot simply dismiss the challenges that come with high-stakes decision-making, tight deadlines, and relentless demands. Managing stress and maintaining razor-sharp focus require innovative strategies and unwavering discipline. There is no magic formula to achieve this, but a combination of time-tested techniques can pave the way for mental clarity and resilience.

First, let's delve into mindfulness and meditation. These practices may seem like buzzwords, but their efficacy is backed by extensive research. Mindfulness allows you to be present, fully engaged with the task at hand. It shifts your focus away from distractions, enabling you to concentrate better. Simple exercises, like focusing on your breath for a few minutes, can significantly reduce stress levels and enhance your concentration. Implementing mindfulness practices in daily routines is not an esoteric pursuit reserved for yogis; it is a powerful strategy for executives seeking clarity amid chaos.

Burnout is a known adversary of productivity and mental well-being. Taking regular breaks and engaging in physical activities are straightforward yet effective ways to combat this. Short breaks during intense work periods help recharge your mental batteries. It sounds counterintuitive, but stepping away from your desk, even for just five minutes, can improve your efficiency and decision-making skills. Physical activities, like walking or light exercises, can act as a reset button for your brain. Movement stimulates the production of endorphins, the body's natural stress relievers, which can help you return to your work with renewed focus and vigor.

Another critical component is time management. Poor time management is a significant stressor. Creating a structured schedule that allocates specific time slots for focused work, meetings, and breaks can drastically reduce stress. Employing tools like calendars, to-do lists, and project management software can aid in organizing tasks efficiently. Prioritizing work based on urgency and importance ensures that you're tackling the most critical tasks first, easing the mental burden and providing a sense of accomplishment.

Learning to say no is an oft-overlooked strategy for managing stress. In the corporate arena, it's easy to become overcommitted. Accepting every request or project can lead to an unmanageable workload and subsequent stress. Establishing boundaries and understanding your limits is crucial. High achievers often fall into the trap of overextending themselves, leading to burnout. Practice assertiveness in your communication, making it clear when you cannot take on additional tasks. By doing so, you can maintain a manageable workload and focus on delivering quality results in your primary responsibilities.

Delegation is another technique that can significantly mitigate stress and enhance focus. Effective leaders understand the value of delegating tasks to qualified team members. Not only does this reduce your workload, but it also empowers others and fosters team collaboration. By entrusting tasks to your team, you free up your time to concentrate on more strategic initiatives and high-priority tasks.

Sleep is perhaps the most natural yet undervalued tool for stress management and focus. The corporate world's culture often glorifies sleepless nights and relentless work hours, but this is a misguided approach. Quality sleep is essential for cognitive functions, including memory, decision-making, and problem-solving skills. Creating a conducive sleep environment, maintaining a consistent sleep schedule, and avoiding stimulants like caffeine before bedtime can improve sleep quality. A well-rested mind is far more capable of handling stress and maintaining focus.

Nutrition plays a pivotal role as well. A balanced diet can impact your mental state and energy levels. Consuming nutrient-rich foods like fruits, vegetables, lean proteins, and whole grains fuels your body and mind, optimizing performance. Avoiding excessive sugar and caffeine, which lead to energy crashes, is equally important. Staying hydrated is another simple yet effective strategy; even mild dehydration can impair cognitive function and increase stress levels.

Social support and networking can serve as valuable buffers against stress. Cultivating strong professional relationships and having a reliable support system can provide emotional support during challenging times. Networking also offers opportunities for collaborative problem-solving and knowledge sharing, reducing feelings of isolation and overwhelm. Engaging in professional communities and seeking mentorship can give you new perspectives, helping you navigate complex corporate landscapes more effectively.

Developing mental resilience is paramount. This involves training your mind to adapt and thrive in challenging environments. Cognitive-behavioral techniques, such as reframing negative thoughts and visualizing success, can alter your perception of stress and enable you to tackle challenges with confidence. Embracing a growth mindset, where you view obstacles as opportunities for learning and improvement, also builds resilience. Such mental conditioning not only helps in managing stress but also enhances your ability to focus on long-term goals amid short-term disruptions.

Lastly, humor can be a powerful antidote to stress. While the corporate world demands seriousness, it doesn't have to be devoid of laughter. Infusing humor into your day can lighten the mental load, making stressful situations more manageable. Laughter triggers the release of endorphins and can instantly boost your mood and reduce stress. Whether it's sharing a light-hearted moment with colleagues or watching a funny video during breaks, humor can act as a mental refresh button, improving your outlook and focus.

In conclusion, managing stress and maintaining focus in the corporate environment requires a multi-faceted approach. Integrating mindfulness, exercise, efficient time management, and proper nutrition into your daily routine can set a strong foundation. Learning to say no, delegating effectively, and developing mental resilience further fortify your ability to handle stress. Cultivating social support and embracing humor adds an additional layer of strength. These strategies, when practiced consistently, can transform your approach to stress and focus, enabling you to excel in the demanding corporate world.

Chapter 4:
Emotional Intelligence in the Corporate Arena

In the fast-paced and often unforgiving corporate environment, emotional intelligence (EI) stands as a cornerstone of effective leadership and critical decision-making. Recognizing and managing one's emotions, while also being attuned to the emotional needs of others, transforms the workplace into a more collaborative and dynamic space. Leaders must navigate the intricate web of interpersonal relationships and communication challenges with finesse and empathy. This ability to connect on an emotional level fosters trust and teamwork, creating an environment where creativity and productivity can flourish. As executives, honing this subtle yet powerful skill not only defines one's professional success but also enriches the broader organizational culture.

Understanding and Managing Emotions

In the fast-paced world of corporate leadership, understanding and managing emotions is not just a valuable asset—it's a critical component of success. Emotions influence decision-making, relationships, and overall performance. A high level of emotional intelligence (EI) can be the distinguishing factor between a good executive and a great one.

At the core of emotional intelligence is self-awareness. This involves recognizing one's own emotional states and understanding the impact they have on thoughts, behaviors, and performance. Self-aware executives can identify triggers that cause stress or anger and respond to them constructively. Becoming self-aware is an ongoing journey that requires reflection and a willingness to assess one's emotional reactions objectively.

Self-awareness naturally leads to self-management. This is the ability to regulate one's emotions, especially in high-pressure situations. For an executive, maintaining composure when faced with challenges is paramount. Self-management includes techniques such as mindfulness, deep breathing exercises, and taking moments of pause before reacting. These practices help reset the mind and keep emotions in check.

Emotional regulation isn't about suppressing emotions but managing them appropriately. For example, turning anxiety into a motivating force or transforming frustration into problem-solving energy. Great leaders harness their emotions to drive positive outcomes, leveraging passion, enthusiasm, and even the occasional nervousness to propel their organizations forward.

Beyond personal emotional regulation, empathy plays a significant role in managing relationships within a corporate setting. Empathy involves understanding and sharing the feelings of others, an ability that enhances communication and fosters stronger relationships. Executives with high empathy can navigate interpersonal dynamics effectively, contribute to a positive organizational culture, and inspire loyalty among team members.

Building strong relationships requires active listening. This means giving full attention to the speaker, acknowledging their feelings, and providing thoughtful feedback. In corporate environments where time is money, it's tempting to rush conversations or multitask during discussions. However, taking the time to listen attentively can resolve conflicts, build trust, and create collaborative opportunities that might otherwise be missed.

Understanding and managing emotions also means recognizing the emotional states of those around you. This is crucial for team management. By being attuned to the emotional climate of the organization, leaders can address concerns before they escalate, ensuring a harmonious working environment. For instance, sensing the early signs of team burnout can prompt timely interventions such as offering breaks, providing additional support, or adjusting workloads.

Creating a culture where emotions are acknowledged and valued can significantly improve team morale. Encouraging open communication about feelings and stressors fosters an inclusive, supportive workplace. This doesn't mean every meeting becomes a therapy session, but rather that there's space for honest, constructive dialogue about emotional well-being.

In managing emotions, it's also essential to set clear, consistent boundaries. Boundaries help define acceptable behaviors and preserve mutual respect. Leaders who model boundary-setting demonstrate a healthy approach to stress management and self-care. It also provides a framework within which team members can understand expectations and feel secure.

Moreover, emotional intelligence encompasses the management of conflict. Conflict is inevitable, but it's how one deals with it that sets effective leaders apart. Addressing conflicts with a balanced perspective—acknowledging emotions while focusing on solutions—leads to resolutions that strengthen rather than fracture relationships. Employing techniques such as "I" statements, active listening, and collaborative problem-solving can turn conflicts into growth opportunities.

Let's consider how emotional intelligence plays out in practical scenarios. Imagine a corporate meeting where tensions are high due to a missed deadline. An executive with high EI would recognize the stress and frustration in the room, address the issue without placing blame, and steer the conversation towards solutions. By doing so, they're not only managing their own emotions but also guiding the team through a potentially disruptive situation.

Developing emotional intelligence in the corporate arena is also about continuous learning and adaptability. Emotional landscapes are dynamic, influenced by both internal and external factors. As such, leaders should continually seek feedback, engage in training, and remain open to personal growth. Books, seminars, and coaching sessions on EI can provide valuable insights and techniques to enhance these skills further.

Importantly, leaders should also practice self-compassion. The corporate world is often unforgiving, with high stakes and relentless demands. Acknowledging one's limitations and not being overly critical of emotional responses is vital. Self-compassion isn't about complacency; it's about recognizing that everyone has flaws and that mistakes are part of the learning process.

Lastly, integrating emotional intelligence into organizational systems can amplify its benefits. This can be achieved by incorporating EI into performance reviews, leadership development programs, and team-building activities. Encouraging an organizational commitment to emotional intelligence will not only improve individual and team performance but also foster a resilient, adaptive corporate culture.

In conclusion, understanding and managing emotions is a multifaceted skill that touches every aspect of corporate life. Self-awareness, self-management, empathy, active listening, conflict resolution, and continuous learning are all integral parts of this process. Executives who master these elements are well-equipped to lead with resilience, foster strong interpersonal relationships, and create an empowering work environment. In the complex and ever-changing corporate arena, emotional intelligence is the cornerstone of enduring success.

Building Strong Relationships and Effective Communication

As we delve deeper into the intricacies of emotional intelligence within the corporate arena, it becomes crucial to understand the significance of building strong relationships and mastering effective communication. In any corporate setting, relationships are the bedrock upon which teamwork, collaboration, and ultimately success are built. Without solid relationships, even the most skilled professionals can find themselves floundering in a sea of misunderstandings and missed opportunities.

One of the first steps in building strong relationships at work is recognizing the importance of genuine connections. People are naturally drawn to those who exude authenticity and show a genuine interest in others. By making a conscious effort to get to know your colleagues beyond their job titles and responsibilities, you lay the foundation for mutual respect and trust. It's not enough to remember birthdays or share pleasantries in the break room; real connections require time, effort, and sometimes vulnerability.

Listening is a cornerstone of any robust relationship. It sounds simple, but effective listening—the kind that makes people feel understood and valued—is a skill that many overlook. Active listening involves not just hearing the words but also interpreting the emotions and intentions behind them. This means putting away distractions, maintaining eye contact, and responding with empathy. When colleagues feel truly heard, they're more likely to reciprocate, creating a cycle of positive communication that benefits everyone.

In addition to listening, clear and concise communication fosters strong relationships. Misunderstandings can lead to conflict and mistrust, which can undermine the foundation of any team or organization. Strive to express your thoughts and ideas clearly, and encourage others to ask questions if something isn't clear. Transparency and openness should be the guiding principles in all your interactions, whether it's a casual conversation at the water cooler or a high-stakes meeting with senior executives.

Another critical aspect of effective communication is adapting your style to suit different personalities and situations. What works with one person may not work with another. Some colleagues may prefer direct, no-nonsense communication, while others might favor a more diplomatic approach. Emotional intelligence involves recognizing these differences and adjusting your communication style accordingly. This flexibility not only aids in delivering your message more effectively but also demonstrates respect for the other person's preferences and comfort zone.

Conflict is inevitable in any dynamic work environment, but it doesn't have to be destructive. When handled thoughtfully, conflicts can actually strengthen relationships by fostering a deeper understanding between parties. The key is to approach conflicts with a problem-solving mindset rather than a confrontational one. Focus on the issue at hand, rather than attacking the individual's character. By demonstrating a willingness to listen and find common ground, you not only resolve the conflict but also build a foundation for stronger, more resilient relationships.

Empathy, often touted as a cornerstone of emotional intelligence, plays a pivotal role in relationship-building. Empathy means putting yourself in someone else's shoes and seeing the world from their perspective. In the corporate context, this could mean understanding the pressures and challenges your colleagues face, recognizing their achievements, and providing support when needed. Displaying empathy can humanize even the most high-pressure environments, making it easier to build connections and work collaboratively towards common goals.

Moreover, mutual respect is a relationship's backbone. Respect isn't just about politeness; it's about valuing each person's contributions and viewpoints. In a diverse corporate environment, different perspectives can lead to innovative solutions, but only if everyone feels respected and heard. Encouraging an inclusive culture where every voice matters can lead to stronger, more cohesive teams that are better equipped to tackle complex challenges.

Effective communication also extends to non-verbal cues. Body language, facial expressions, and even the tone of your voice can communicate volumes more than words alone. Being mindful of these non-verbal signals helps you convey your message more accurately and interpret the unspoken feelings of others. For instance, an open posture can indicate receptiveness, while crossed arms might signal defensiveness or discomfort. By being aware of these cues, you can adjust your own behavior and responses to foster better understanding and rapport.

In today's digital age, communication isn't confined to face-to-face interactions. Emails, instant messaging, and virtual meetings are ubiquitous in the corporate world. While these tools offer convenience, they also present their own set of challenges. Misinterpretations are more likely when the nuances of tone and body language are stripped away. Therefore, it's essential to be even more meticulous in your digital communications. Clear, concise, and well-thought-out messages can prevent misunderstandings and ensure that your intent is accurately conveyed.

Trust is the glue that holds organizational relationships together, and it's built through consistent, reliable, and honest communication. When you follow through on your commitments and communicate openly about challenges and setbacks, you build a reputation for integrity. This, in turn, makes others more likely to trust you, creating a positive feedback loop of trust and reliability. Remember, trust is hard to build but easy to lose, so every interaction counts.

Finally, fostering a positive work environment can significantly impact relationship-building and communication. When people feel happy and valued at work, they're more likely to engage positively with their colleagues. Celebrating achievements, providing constructive feedback, and encouraging a culture of continuous improvement can boost morale and create a sense of community. In such an environment, strong relationships and effective communication naturally flourish.

In conclusion, building strong relationships and effective communication are not just desirable traits but critical components of emotional intelligence in the corporate arena. They require a combination of skills, strategies, and a deep understanding of human behavior. By focusing on genuine connections, active listening, clear expression, adaptability, and empathy, you lay the groundwork for a successful and fulfilling career. The effort you put into cultivating these relationships will pay dividends in the form of a supportive, collaborative, and ultimately high-performing work environment.

Chapter 5:
Time Management and Productivity

Time management and productivity form the backbone of any successful corporate executive's arsenal. Without a firm grasp on how to prioritize tasks and set realistic yet challenging goals, even the most talented professionals can find themselves overwhelmed and underperforming. Developing effective techniques for maximizing efficiency involves not just a keen awareness of one's daily schedule but also an understanding of the broader strategic objectives that drive the organization forward. The ability to delegate, eliminate distractions, and focus on high-impact activities will separate the exceptional leaders from the rest. As you hone these skills, you'll find that increased productivity not only enhances your performance but also contributes to a more balanced and fulfilling career. This chapter delves into the art and science of managing your most valuable resource—time—and offers practical strategies to elevate your productivity to new heights.

Prioritizing Tasks and Setting Goals

Effective time management is central to the success of any corporate executive. When juggling multiple responsibilities and high-stakes projects, mastering the art of prioritizing tasks and setting goals becomes not just useful but essential. The ability to clearly define what needs to be done and to establish a plan to achieve it allows executives to maintain focus, delegate work efficiently, and ultimately achieve their objectives.

From ordinary to extraordinary

Prioritizing tasks starts with understanding what truly matters. As an executive, not every email, meeting, or report demands your immediate attention. It's crucial to first recognize what is urgent versus what is important. Urgent tasks require immediate action and often relate to crisis management or tight deadlines, whereas important tasks contribute more directly to your long-term goals and success. Stephen Covey's Time Management Matrix can be a helpful tool here — categorize tasks into four quadrants based on their urgency and importance.

One effective method to identify and prioritize these tasks is the Eisenhower Box, which divides tasks into four categories: Do First (urgent and important), Schedule (important but not urgent), Delegate (urgent but not important), and Don't Do (neither urgent nor important). This approach helps in not only organizing tasks but also in making quick decisions on what needs your attention now and what can wait or be passed to someone else.

Once tasks are prioritized, setting clear, achievable goals becomes the next critical step. Goals provide direction and a sense of purpose, aligning day-to-day activities with broader objectives. When setting goals, follow the SMART criteria: Specific, Measurable, Achievable, Relevant, and Time-bound. This method ensures that your goals are clear and attainable, providing a roadmap for success. Instead of saying, "improve sales," a more effective goal would be, "Increase sales by 15% in the next quarter by improving client relationships and enhancing product features."

To maintain a steady progress towards these goals, break them down into smaller, manageable tasks or milestones. This makes large goals less daunting and keeps you motivated by allowing frequent wins. Using project management tools like Asana or Trello can help track these smaller tasks and ensure nothing falls through the cracks.

Even the most well-laid plans encounter obstacles, and flexibility is key. As demands shift and new priorities emerge, adapt your plan accordingly. Periodically review and adjust your task lists and goals to reflect changing circumstances. Regular reflection not only keeps you on track but also offers the opportunity to celebrate progress and recalibrate strategies.

Time blocking is another powerful technique for managing both priority tasks and goals. Allocate specific blocks of time for focused work on high-priority tasks. During these blocks, minimize distractions and concentrate solely on the task at hand. This method, sometimes linked with the Pomodoro Technique, promotes deep work and can significantly enhance productivity.

Effective delegation cannot be overlooked in this context. As an executive, it's vital to empower your team by delegating tasks that don't require your direct oversight. Delegation should be strategic, with tasks assigned based on team members' strengths and workloads. This not only frees up your time for higher-level priorities but also helps in building a competent and motivated team.

Finally, aligning your tasks and goals with the broader vision of the organization ensures that your efforts contribute to collective success. Regularly communicate with your team and stakeholders to stay in sync and adjust your priorities as necessary to support the company's objectives.

In conclusion, the interplay of prioritizing tasks and setting goals is a dynamic process that requires ongoing assessment and adaptation. With these strategies, you can better manage your responsibilities, lead your team effectively, and drive the organization towards its goals, reaffirming your role as a successful corporate executive.

Techniques for Maximizing Efficiency

Time is the ultimate resource, and managing it effectively is the hallmark of any successful executive. When it comes to maximizing efficiency, the truth lies not just in doing things right but in doing the right things. The corporate world is a maelstrom of responsibilities, deadlines, and distractions. Therefore, adopting and mastering specific techniques can propel you ahead of your peers, setting a robust precedent for achieving productivity.

One fundamental approach to maximizing efficiency is leveraging the **Eisenhower Matrix**. This framework helps you prioritize tasks by categorizing them into four quadrants based on urgency and importance. By focusing primarily on activities that are both important and urgent, you mitigate the risks associated with procrastination and last-minute rushes. This quadrant-based strategy is more than just a theoretical exercise; it brings clarity to your daily regimen, allowing you to clearly see where your time will deliver the most impact.

Equally significant is the practice of *time blocking*. Time blocking involves the division of your day into distinct chunks, each dedicated to specific tasks or types of work. By committing dedicated intervals to high-priority activities, you create an environment that minimizes interruptions and distractions. Moreover, this method enables you to enter a state of deep work, which has been proven to significantly enhance productivity.

Employing the **Pomodoro Technique** can also yield remarkable results. This technique encourages work in 25-minute increments, followed by short breaks. Three to four such intervals are then succeeded by a longer break, which provides ample time for mental recovery. The rationale behind this method is simple yet powerful: breaking tasks into smaller, manageable units makes them less daunting and increases focus.

Automation should not be overlooked when discussing efficiency. Leveraging technology to automate repetitive and mundane tasks can free up substantial time, allowing you to focus on tasks that require critical thinking and decision-making. Whether it's using software to manage emails or delegating routine administrative tasks through AI, automation is a vital cog in the efficiency machine.

To amplify your efficiency further, embrace the "Two-Minute Rule." If a task takes less than two minutes to complete, do it immediately. This rule reduces the buildup of small tasks that can otherwise consume considerable time when left unaddressed. Quick wins also generate a sense of accomplishment, which can boost motivation and productivity.

Moreover, batch processing similar tasks can streamline your workflow. Responding to emails, making phone calls, or even scheduling meetings in dedicated blocks ensures that you remain focused and reduces the cognitive load associated with constantly switching between different types of activities. Batch processing maximizes efficiency by optimizing your mental and physical energy.

Understanding your *peak performance windows* is also crucial. These are periods during the day when you are naturally more alert, focused, and energized. Identifying and scheduling high-stakes tasks during these windows can significantly enhance your productivity. Conversely, allocating routine tasks to less productive periods ensures that your prime hours are used effectively.

Let's also discuss the significance of delegation. Recognizing that you can't do everything yourself is paramount for efficient time management. Delegating tasks not only allows you to focus on high-value activities but also empowers your team members, fostering a culture of trust and collaboration. Effective delegation involves clear communication and follow-up to ensure tasks are completed to the required standard.

Another subtle yet powerful technique involves establishing a "Getting Ready Ritual." This entails setting aside time at the beginning of your day to align your focus, establish your priorities, and set your intentions. A well-defined morning routine can set the tone for the rest of the day, fostering a disciplined and proactive mindset.

To further enhance efficiency, cultivate the habit of reflecting on your performance. At the end of each day, take a few minutes to review what you've accomplished, identify areas for improvement, and adjust your plans accordingly. This reflective practice creates a feedback loop, enabling you to continuously refine your strategies and performance.

Setting SMART goals—Specific, Measurable, Achievable, Relevant, and Time-bound—is another cornerstone of maximizing efficiency. Clearly defined objectives provide direction and purpose, enabling you to allocate your time and resources effectively. Regularly reviewing and adjusting your goals ensures they remain aligned with your broader objectives and priorities.

Equally invaluable is the practice of eliminating time-wasters. Identifying habits or activities that consume time without adding value is critical. Whether it's excessive social media use, unproductive meetings, or prolonged discussions, being conscious of these time-wasting elements and taking steps to mitigate them can significantly increase your efficiency.

Another potent technique involves limiting multitasking. Contrary to popular belief, multitasking often diminishes productivity and increases the likelihood of errors. Focusing on one task at a time allows for deeper concentration and higher-quality results. It's a simple yet effective strategy for maintaining efficiency in a fast-paced corporate environment.

Finally, but certainly not least, investing in personal well-being cannot be overstated. Ensuring adequate sleep, nutrition, and physical exercise are foundational to maintaining high levels of productivity. A well-rested body and a nourished mind are far more effective than one operating on fumes. Balancing work with adequate rest and recreation is pivotal in sustaining peak performance.

In conclusion, while the techniques for maximizing efficiency are interwoven with individual habits and inclinations, their synergistic application can create a powerful framework for exceptional productivity. By integrating these strategies into your daily routine, you establish a robust foundation for continuous success in the corporate world. As you navigate through the complexities of executive life, these time-tested techniques can not only enhance your productivity but also contribute to a more balanced and fulfilling professional journey.

Chapter 6:
Leadership and Team Dynamics

In the corporate world, effective leadership and a keen understanding of team dynamics are paramount to success. A leader's vision, along with their ability to inspire and motivate, can propel a team to new heights, fostering not only productivity but also a shared sense of purpose. Effective leaders exhibit traits such as integrity, decisiveness, and empathy, creating an environment where trust and collaboration can flourish. However, great leadership extends beyond personal attributes; it's about nurturing a culture that values every team member's contribution, encouraging innovation, and fostering resilience. Building and leading high-performance teams involve recognizing individual strengths, facilitating open communication, and ensuring that every team member feels valued and empowered to contribute their best. In essence, true leadership is about striking a balance between guiding the team with a clear vision and adapting to the dynamic needs of the corporate landscape.

Traits of Effective Leaders

Effective leadership is a cornerstone of successful team dynamics and corporate success. It's not merely about wielding authority or delegating tasks. Rather, it's about embodying a series of traits that inspire, motivate, and drive both individuals and teams towards excellence. A dynamic leader can transform challenges into opportunities, foster a cohesive culture, and drive the organization towards achieving its strategic goals.

First and foremost, an effective leader must possess **vision**. This isn't just about setting goals but about seeing the bigger picture and having a long-term perspective. They visualize not only where the organization should go, but also understand the steps needed to get there. Visionary leaders are able to articulate this vision clearly, ensuring their teams understand and align with it. They inspire with a clear direction, and their foresight allows them to anticipate challenges that may lie ahead.

In tandem with vision is the necessity for **communication skills**. A leader must be proficient in both verbal and written communication. Open and transparent communication fosters trust within the team. Moreover, effective leaders are active listeners. They don't just hear their team members but genuinely understand their concerns and ideas. This two-way communication ensures that everyone feels heard and valued, which can significantly boost morale and collaboration.

Another indispensable trait is **integrity**. Trust is the bedrock of any relationship, and it's no different in a corporate setting. Leaders who demonstrate integrity are consistent in their actions, values, and decisions. They stick to their principles, even when it's challenging. This not only earns them the respect of their peers and subordinates but also sets a standard for the entire organization. Integrity-driven leaders create a culture where ethical behavior is the norm, not the exception.

Being an effective leader also means having a high degree of **emotional intelligence** (EI). This involves understanding one's own emotions and managing them effectively while also being attuned to the emotions of others. Leaders with high EI are empathetic and recognize the emotional undercurrents within their team, addressing tensions before they escalate. Such leaders can navigate the complexities of interpersonal relationships skillfully, ensuring a harmonious and productive work environment.

Moreover, effective leaders are adept at **decision-making**. They must efficiently analyze information, weigh pros and cons, and make sound judgments. This doesn't mean they're infallible; rather, they are willing to make difficult decisions and take responsibility for the outcomes. They also foster a decision-making environment where team members feel empowered to contribute, promoting a culture of shared responsibility.

Adaptability is another trait that can't be understated. The corporate landscape is ever-evolving, and a leader must be flexible and open to change. They should be proactive in seeking out new opportunities and innovative solutions. Adaptable leaders are not thrown off course by unexpected challenges; instead, they pivot and find new pathways to success. This resilience inspires confidence and encourages a similar attitude among team members.

Empowerment is a trait that truly differentiates leaders from managers. Effective leaders cultivate potential within their team, providing opportunities for growth and development. They entrust team members with responsibility and encourage autonomy. This empowerment not only boosts confidence but also drives greater ownership and accountability, leading to higher performance levels.

Equally important is the trait of **humility**. Effective leaders recognize that they don't have all the answers and are open to learning from others. They acknowledge their team's contributions and are not afraid to admit their mistakes. This humility creates an environment where continuous feedback and improvement are encouraged, fostering a culture of mutual respect and trust.

Resilience is a crucial trait for navigating the inevitable ups and downs in the corporate world. Leaders must maintain their composure in the face of adversity and be unwavering in their commitment to their vision. Their ability to stay positive and persistent, even in challenging times, serves as a beacon of strength for their team.

Lastly, an effective leader must demonstrate **inspirational motivation**. They need to inspire and motivate their team to exceed their potential. This involves not only setting high standards but also recognizing and celebrating achievements, big and small. By fostering a sense of purpose and passion, leaders can ignite the drive within their team, leading to unprecedented levels of engagement and performance.

In summary, effective leadership transcends simple task management. It's about embodying qualities that evoke trust, inspire vision, and drive the collective towards success. Leaders who master these traits can cultivate an environment where individuals and teams thrive, driving the organization to new heights. By understanding and practicing these traits, one can truly excel in the complex and dynamic world of corporate leadership.

Building and Leading High-Performance Teams

Creating and steering high-performance teams is an art that requires not only strategy but also a deep understanding of human dynamics. Effective leadership is at the heart of this endeavor, entailing a blend of vision, empathy, and relentless commitment. In the high-stakes corporate environment, where competition is fierce and time is ever scarce, the ability to mold and lead a team to excellence can often spell the difference between success and failure.

Leadership starts with a clear vision. To build a high-performance team, a leader must articulate a compelling vision that resonates deeply with every team member. This vision should transcend monetary goals and appeal to a collective sense of purpose. When a team shares a united vision, it galvanizes their efforts and fosters a collaborative spirit, vital for achieving sustainable success.

Equally crucial is the development of trust and mutual respect. High-performance teams thrive in environments where members feel valued and trusted. Delegating responsibilities while allowing autonomy can empower team members and prompt innovation. Micromanagement, on the other hand, often stifles creativity and demoralizes team members. By offering support and guidance rather than control, leaders enable their teams to grow and contribute meaningfully.

Communication is another cornerstone. Open, honest, and transparent communication helps in building trust and addressing issues before they escalate. Regular team meetings and one-on-one sessions provide platforms for feedback, recognition, and realignment. Leaders should listen actively, acknowledging concerns and values while fostering an environment where everyone feels heard.

However, vision and communication alone are not enough. Implementing structured processes and strategies is essential for converting ideas into action. This includes setting clear, achievable goals and defining roles and responsibilities. High-performance teams need a roadmap that outlines the pathway to success and provides milestones for assessing progress. Leaders must also be flexible, ready to adapt strategies as new challenges and opportunities arise.

A focus on continuous improvement distinguishes high-performing teams from the rest. Encouraging a culture of learning and development ensures that team skills remain sharp and relevant. Leaders should create opportunities for professional growth through training, workshops, and access to educational resources. By investing in their team's development, leaders not only enhance individual capabilities but also reinforce the collective strength of the team.

Emotional intelligence plays a significant role in team dynamics. Leaders adept in emotional intelligence can navigate the complexities of interpersonal relationships with finesse. They can identify and manage their own emotions while understanding and influencing the emotions of others. This skill is vital for resolving conflicts, understanding team dynamics, and motivating individuals under varying circumstances. Leaders with high emotional intelligence can maintain a cohesive and harmonious team environment even in the face of adversity.

Recognition and rewards are powerful motivators. Recognizing individual and team accomplishments fosters a sense of achievement and encourages a culture of excellence. Acknowledgment should be authentic and specific, celebrating not only the notable successes but also the consistent efforts that contribute to the team's overall performance. By highlighting different types of contributions, leaders can ensure that recognition is inclusive and comprehensive.

The diversity of thought is another invaluable asset in high-performance teams. Encouraging diversity of opinions and perspectives leads to richer discussions and innovative solutions. Leaders should consciously cultivate an inclusive environment where every team member feels comfortable expressing their ideas and perspectives. By leveraging the diverse strengths and experiences of the team, leaders can drive creativity and innovation.

Conflict, though often perceived negatively, can be a catalyst for growth when managed properly. Leaders must address conflicts promptly and constructively, transforming potential disruptions into opportunities for improvement. By facilitating open dialogues and promoting resolution strategies, leaders can eliminate friction and steer the team towards a more cohesive and productive state.

Lastly, resilience is a hallmark of high-performance teams. Setbacks and failures are inevitable, but resilient teams possess the grit to navigate through challenges and bounce back stronger. Leaders play a crucial role in nurturing this resilience by maintaining a positive outlook, encouraging a problem-solving mindset, and offering steadfast support during difficult times.

Building and leading high-performance teams is an ongoing journey, requiring patience, dedication, and a nuanced understanding of both strategy and human nature. Weaving together vision, trust, communication, structure, continuous improvement, emotional intelligence, recognition, diversity, conflict resolution, and resilience, leaders can guide their teams to achieve extraordinary results. Through intentional and empathetic leadership, the potential of every team can be unlocked, setting the stage for remarkable accomplishments in the corporate arena.

Chapter 7: Continuous Learning and Adaptability

In the ever-evolving landscape of the corporate world, continuous learning and adaptability aren't just assets—they're essential survival tools. Corporations today demand executives who are not only adept in their current skills but also agile enough to master new ones swiftly. This ongoing commitment to learning fuels innovation, keeping leaders ahead of industry shifts and technological advancements. It's about cultivating a mindset that embraces change rather than fears it, seeing every challenge as an opportunity to grow. Adaptability allows one to pivot strategies when old methods don't suffice, ensuring sustained relevance and competence. To thrive, executives must constantly seek knowledge, remain flexible, and be prepared to reinvent themselves when necessary. The ability to adapt in such a dynamic environment distinguishes true leaders from the rest, marking the difference between those who merely cope and those who excel.

The Importance of Lifelong Learning

In navigating the intricate labyrinth of the corporate world, there's one principle that stands tall amongst others: the commitment to lifelong learning. Far beyond the bounds of academic classrooms, this notion stretches infinitely, shaping and reshaping an executive throughout their career. To truly excel as a corporate leader, one must embrace this tenet with fervor, forever seeking knowledge, understanding, and growth.

From ordinary to extraordinary

Lifelong learning is not a new concept, but its importance in the modern corporate environment can't be overstated. In an era where technology and market trends evolve at breakneck speed, an executive who remains static risks becoming obsolete. The best leaders are those who intentionally cultivate an insatiable hunger for knowledge. They don't rely solely on their past experiences or degrees; instead, they immerse themselves in continuous education, be it through formal training or self-directed learning.

Consider the case of a seasoned executive who began their career in the pre-digital era. The skills and strategies that led to success three decades ago likely have little relevance today. Technology has transformed the way we communicate, analyze data, and even manage teams. For such an executive to continue thriving, they must invest time in understanding new tools, platforms, and methodologies. Lifelong learning, in this context, is both a shield and a sword – offering protection against obsolescence and the capability to seize new opportunities.

But it's not just about keeping up with technological advancements. Lifelong learning encompasses a broad spectrum of knowledge areas. Organizational behavior, cultural competence, market dynamics, and ethical leadership – these are fields that constantly evolve. An adaptive executive continuously seeks to understand how these areas intersect with their role and influence their decisions.

Moreover, lifelong learning fosters personal growth beyond mere professional development. It encourages introspection and self-awareness. By engaging in learning activities, whether reading the latest industry books or attending seminars, executives often find themselves reflecting on their own beliefs and biases. This process of self-examination can lead to profound personal transformation, enhancing one's ability to lead with empathy and authenticity.

Lifelong learning also instills a mindset of humility. No matter how experienced or knowledgeable, there's always something new to learn – a novel perspective to consider or an innovative solution to explore. This humility can be a powerful leadership trait, fostering a collaborative environment where team members feel valued and heard. It can transform organizational culture, paving the way for collective growth and shared achievements.

Mentorship and coaching play pivotal roles in promoting lifelong learning. As leaders, executives have the responsibility not only to cultivate their own growth but also to foster a culture that encourages continuous learning within their teams. By mentoring younger professionals or seeking mentorship from peers and industry leaders, executives can exchange knowledge, inspire innovation, and uplift the entire organization. This cycle of giving and receiving wisdom enriches the professional journey of all involved.

Incorporating lifelong learning into one's career requires intention and strategic planning. It is essential to set aside dedicated time for learning amidst the pressing demands of corporate responsibilities. Scheduling regular intervals for reading industry reports, participating in webinars, or enrolling in online courses can make a substantial difference. Additionally, joining professional networks and attending conferences can provide insights into emerging trends and technologies, enhancing an executive's ability to adapt and lead effectively.

"Adaptability is key." This adage resonates deeply within the context of lifelong learning. The ability to pivot strategies, embrace changes, and overcome unforeseen challenges is what sets extraordinary leaders apart from the rest. In times of crisis or rapid transformation, those who have invested in continuous learning are better equipped to navigate uncertainties and steer their organizations toward success. They are the ones who see opportunities where others see obstacles, thanks to their broad knowledge base and adaptable mindset.

Take, for instance, the disruptive impact of a global pandemic. Executives who devoted themselves to a culture of lifelong learning found themselves prepared to shift their operations, embrace remote work models, and explore new revenue streams. Their familiarity with digital tools, agile methodologies, and resilience-building techniques empowered them to lead with confidence and compassion during turbulent times. This adaptability didn't emerge overnight; it was the fruit of consistent, intentional learning.

To solidify the importance of lifelong learning, one must view it as a vital component of strategic planning. Companies that prioritize continuous education for their leaders witness long-term benefits, such as increased innovation, enhanced employee morale, and sustained competitive advantage. A leadership team that values and practices lifelong learning sets the stage for a dynamic, forward-thinking corporate ethos.

The journey of lifelong learning is not a solitary endeavor. Building a network of peers, mentors, and industry experts can enrich the learning experience. Collaborative learning environments, where ideas and knowledge are shared freely, can be fertile grounds for innovation and breakthroughs. Engaging in discussions, debates, and collaborative projects with colleagues from diverse backgrounds can expand one's horizons, fostering a deeper understanding of global business dynamics.

Certainly, it's not purely the acquisition of new knowledge that defines lifelong learning but also the application of that knowledge. Executives must translate their learning into actionable strategies, driving tangible results and inspiring their teams. This practical approach not only reinforces the value of continuous education but also demonstrates leadership by example, reinforcing a culture of lifelong learning within the organization.

In summary, the importance of lifelong learning in the corporate world cannot be overstated. It is the cornerstone of continuous personal and professional growth, enabling executives to remain relevant, adaptable, and resilient amidst ever-evolving challenges. By committing to a lifelong journey of learning, corporate leaders can unlock their full potential, inspire their teams, and drive their organizations toward enduring success. The quest for knowledge is infinite, and those who embrace it wholeheartedly will find themselves at the pinnacle of corporate excellence.

Adapting to Change in the Corporate World

The ability to adapt to change is one of the most crucial skills a corporate executive can develop. Change, often unpredictable and sometimes unwelcome, is a constant in the corporate world. Those who thrive learn to see change not as a threat but as an opportunity for growth and innovation. Embracing this mindset can transform challenges into stepping stones and obstacles into learning experiences.

Successful corporate executives understand that adaptability is not just about reacting to changes; it's about anticipating them. This forward-thinking approach requires a continuous investment in learning. The landscape of the corporate world is in perpetual motion, driven by technological advancements, market dynamics, and evolving consumer behaviors. Staying ahead means constantly updating one's knowledge and skills, ensuring they remain relevant and competitive.

One key aspect of adapting to change is fostering a growth mindset. This concept, popularized by psychologist Carol Dweck, emphasizes the belief that abilities and intelligence can be developed through dedication and hard work. A growth mindset cultivates resilience, encouraging individuals to embrace challenges, persist through setbacks, and view effort as a path to mastery. Corporate executives with a growth mindset are more likely to perceive change as an opportunity to learn and grow, rather than a disruptive force.

Another essential element is the willingness to leave one's comfort zone. Comfort zones, while safe and familiar, can become stifling over time. They can hinder progress and limit potential. Executives who push past these boundaries develop a sense of flexibility and robustness. This flexibility equips them to handle diverse situations, make quick decisions, and implement innovative strategies. Venturing beyond comfort zones may involve taking on new roles, exploring unfamiliar markets, or engaging in continuous professional development.

Adaptability also involves understanding the broader context in which changes occur. Executives need to stay informed about industry trends, economic shifts, and societal changes. This knowledge enables them to make informed decisions and strategically guide their organizations through periods of transition. Keeping a finger on the pulse of these factors is not a one-time task; it requires ongoing attention and curiosity.

Networking plays a pivotal role in adapting to change. Building and maintaining a robust professional network can provide insights, support, and opportunities that are invaluable during times of change. Networking isn't just about exchanging business cards; it's about forging meaningful relationships. Engaging with peers, mentors, and industry leaders can offer diverse perspectives and foster a collaborative environment where collective learning and problem-solving thrive.

In addition to external networks, internal company culture significantly influences adaptability. A culture that encourages experimentation, welcomes feedback, and rewards innovation can empower employees at all levels to embrace change. Executives must champion such a culture, leading by example and fostering an environment where team members feel safe to take calculated risks and explore new ideas.

Adapting to change also necessitates robust emotional intelligence. Change often brings uncertainty and stress, which can affect morale and productivity. Executives who are attuned to their own emotions and the emotions of others can navigate these challenges more effectively. They can provide the support and reassurance needed to guide their teams through transitions, maintaining a positive and productive work environment.

Moreover, the ability to prioritize is crucial. Changes, particularly those in rapid succession, can overwhelm even the most seasoned professionals. Executives must develop the skill to discern which changes require immediate attention and which can be deferred. This triage approach ensures that resources are allocated efficiently and critical issues are addressed promptly.

Regular reflection and feedback are fundamental to continuous learning and adaptability. Reflection allows executives to evaluate their responses to changes, learn from their experiences, and identify areas for improvement. Similarly, seeking feedback from peers, mentors, and team members provides external perspectives that can reveal blind spots and highlight strengths. Both practices foster a continuous cycle of growth and development.

Technology, with its rapid advancement, plays a dual role in change. It can be both a catalyst for and a solution to the challenges posed by change. Executives must stay abreast of technological innovations and consider how these advancements can be integrated into their strategies. Leveraging technology can streamline processes, enhance communication, and provide data-driven insights that inform decision-making. However, technology should be seen as a tool, not a crutch. The human element, characterized by creativity, critical thinking, and emotional intelligence, remains irreplaceable.

Ultimately, adapting to change in the corporate world requires a holistic approach. This involves cultivating a mindset that welcomes learning, embracing the discomfort of leaving one's comfort zone, understanding the broader context of change, fostering strong networks, championing a supportive organizational culture, prioritizing effectively, reflecting regularly, and leveraging technology. By integrating these elements into their professional lives, corporate executives can navigate the ever-evolving landscape with confidence and competence.

In conclusion, adaptability is not a static skill but a dynamic process that requires ongoing effort and commitment. As executives, the ability to adapt to change not only enhances personal growth but also drives organizational success. By embracing change as an integral part of the corporate journey, executives can lead with agility and resilience, turning challenges into opportunities for innovation and excellence.

Chapter 8:
Crafting Your Personal Brand

As we navigate our corporate journeys, crafting a personal brand becomes a non-negotiable asset for career success. Think of your personal brand as your unique fingerprint in the professional world—one that needs careful shaping and polishing to make a lasting impression. This involves understanding your unique value proposition, which sets you apart from the crowd, and proactively gathering feedback to grasp how others perceive you. By constructing a compelling personal narrative and strategically enhancing your online presence, you lay the foundations of an authentic and memorable identity. Further, leveraging public speaking and writing not only amplifies your voice but also establishes you as a thought leader in your field. Remember, your personal brand isn't just about who you are today but who you're aspiring to become, and every interaction is a step in solidifying that vision.

Identifying Your Unique Value Proposition

In the labyrinth of corporate life, standing out can seem like an insurmountable challenge. Yet, there's a way to ensure you're more than just a face in the crowd: by identifying your unique value proposition (UVP). Your UVP is that special blend of strengths, values, and experiences that sets you apart from others. It's your unique cocktail of skills and qualities, distilled from a lifetime of personal and professional growth. It's the key to unlocking doors, seizing opportunities, and propelling your career forward.

Start by considering your strengths. These are the innate talents and acquired skills that you bring to the table. They're the things you excel at, perhaps the tasks others struggle with but you find almost effortless. Reflect on moments in your career when you've felt particularly successful or proud. What were you doing? Why were you good at it? Were you utilizing strategic thinking, exceptional communication, or perhaps a knack for innovation? Recognizing your strengths is the first step toward articulating your unique value proposition.

Your values play a crucial role in shaping your UVP. They act as guiding principles, influencing your decisions and actions in both professional and personal realms. Your values could encompass integrity, dedication, teamwork, or even a commitment to continuous learning. When your values align with your actions, you operate at your most authentic and effective level. More importantly, they resonate with others, including colleagues, leaders, and clients. Think about what matters most to you and how these principles manifest in your daily work life.

Experiences, both triumphant and challenging, also form a critical element of your proposition. Your career journey, the roles you've held, the projects you've led or participated in, and even the setbacks you've overcome, all contribute to your unique narrative. Perhaps you've navigated a failing project to success, or you've introduced a groundbreaking process that increased efficiency. These experiences demonstrate resilience, adaptability, and an ability to innovate, all valuable traits in a corporate executive.

Consider Susan, a project manager in a tech company. Early in her career, she realized her knack for navigating complex projects and her passion for technology. Her strengths in analytical thinking and team management were complemented by her values of transparency and excellence. Over the years, she logged experiences that ranged from successful product launches to navigating company-wide system overhauls. By combining these elements, Susan's UVP became clear: she was a tech-savvy leader adept at steering projects through turbulent waters to successful outcomes.

Identifying your UVP also means understanding your market. In the corporate world, your market is your workplace and industry. Consider the demands and challenges of your current role and sector. What are the pressing needs? What gaps can you fill? This step ensures that your proposition isn't just unique but also relevant and valuable. For instance, if you're in a rapidly evolving industry like tech, emphasizing adaptability and innovation in your UVP can be crucial.

It's also beneficial to compare your UVP with peers and mentors. Not to mimic theirs, but to understand the nuances that make yours distinct. Engaging in this comparative analysis might reveal insights you hadn't considered about your own value proposition. You can also gather feedback to see how others perceive your strengths, values, and experiences. Sometimes, others can see our unique value more clearly than we can ourselves.

Your UVP is not static; it evolves as you grow professionally and personally. Regular introspection and reassessment ensure that it stays aligned with your career progression and aspirations. Take time periodically to reflect on what new strengths have emerged, any shifts in your core values, and recent experiences that have shaped you. Keeping your UVP updated ensures it remains a true and effective representation of who you are and what you offer.

Crafting your UVP isn't just about self-awareness; it is about self-promotion, in the best possible sense. Once identified, integrate it into every aspect of your professional life. Your resume should reflect it, your LinkedIn profile should boast of it, and your daily interactions should subtly echo it. This consistency will reinforce your brand in the minds of others, making you a memorable and compelling figure in your field.

In conclusion, your unique value proposition is a dynamic amalgamation of your strengths, values, and experiences. It's what makes you irreplaceable and vital in your professional environment. By understanding and clearly articulating your UVP, you position yourself not just as another employee but as a unique asset to any team or organization. Embrace this process of self-discovery and watch as it opens doors and propels you to new heights in your corporate journey.

Gathering Feedback to Understand How Others Perceive You

Crafting a personal brand isn't a solitary endeavor. It's a dynamic process that involves an interplay between one's self-perception and how others view you. Gathering feedback is crucial in this regard. Without an understanding of external perceptions, your personal brand may be anchored in your internal biases and misaligned with the expectations of your professional landscape.

Begin by actively seeking feedback from a diverse cross-section of individuals in your professional network. These should include mentors, peers, subordinates, and even clients if possible. It's equally important to consider both formal and informal channels for collecting this feedback. A structured performance review at work, for instance, is an invaluable formal resource, but impromptu conversations can yield insights that formal mechanisms might miss. Ask specific questions that solicit actionable feedback, such as "What are my strengths?" and "In which areas could I improve?"

Feedback should never be viewed as a criticism of your character but as a constructive insight into your professional effectiveness. The distinction is vital; it equips you to objectively evaluate areas needing development while reinforcing your strengths. One must approach feedback with a growth mindset—embracing it as an opportunity to evolve continually.

Sometimes, feedback can be contradictory. One colleague might applaud you for your attention to detail, while another could perceive it as micromanaging. In these cases, look for patterns rather than anomalies. Consistent feedback across different sources is generally more reflective of genuine strengths or areas for improvement. If discrepancies arise, consider the context and the individual providing the feedback. Their relationship with you and their own professional experiences can color their perception.

Construct a feedback loop. After collating inputs, devote time to analyze and implement changes. Regularly revisit the same people to assess if their perception has shifted following your adjustments. This iterative process underscores your commitment to self-improvement and demonstrates a high degree of professionalism.

A balanced personal brand reflects not only who you are but also how you are perceived. Misalignment between self-perception and external perception can result in miscommunications and missed opportunities. One practical approach is to develop a "360-degree feedback" practice within your organization. This method encourages feedback from all angles, providing a holistic view of how you're perceived within the corporate ecosystem.

Utilize digital tools and platforms for anonymous feedback, as anonymity can encourage candid responses. Tools such as Surveymonkey or Google Forms allow you to create comprehensive questionnaires without revealing the identity of respondents. This ensures the feedback is uninfluenced by personal relationships and positions within the company.

Additionally, consider engaging in peer review practices. Form a small group of trusted colleagues who periodically review each other's professional performance. The reciprocal nature of this practice fosters a supportive environment conducive to honest and constructive feedback.

In conclusion, gathering feedback to understand how others perceive you is not merely an exercise but a pivotal element in crafting a robust personal brand. The journey demands an open mind, a willingness to evolve, and a systematic approach to integrating diverse perspectives. By embedding these practices into your professional routine, you ensure your personal brand is not only self-assured but also aligned with the broader expectations and realities of your corporate environment.

Creating a Compelling Personal Narrative

Crafting a strong personal narrative is at the heart of building a memorable and effective personal brand. Your narrative is more than just a collection of facts about where you've been and what you've achieved. It's a coherent and compelling story that aligns with your professional goals, resonates with colleagues and clients, and guides your career trajectory.

First and foremost, to create a compelling personal narrative, you need to reflect on key moments in your career that have shaped you. These can be triumphs, challenges, or even failures that taught you invaluable lessons. Reflect on how these experiences have molded your skills, attitude, and approach to your profession. Perhaps it was a challenging project that taught you the importance of resilience and adaptability, or maybe it was a collaboration that underscored the value of effective communication. Identifying these pivotal moments is crucial because they form the backbone of your narrative and make it authentic and relatable.

Next, consider how these experiences align with your present professional goals. Ask yourself what themes consistently emerge from your career story. Are you someone who thrives in solving complex problems? Do you excel in building and leading high-performance teams? Recognizing these patterns can help you pinpoint your unique strengths and areas of expertise, which are essential in articulating a narrative that resonates with others.

Your personal narrative should not only focus on the past and present but also cast a vision for the future. This forward-looking perspective inspires and motivates both you and your audience. If you're aspiring to take on leadership roles, for instance, your narrative should weave in your plans to develop leadership skills and the impact you aim to make. It's about crafting a story that's not static but dynamic and evolving.

A vital aspect of your narrative is its emotional appeal. Human experiences and emotions connect us in ways that dry, factual details cannot. Therefore, infuse your narrative with personal anecdotes, heartfelt reflections, and genuine insights. For example, instead of merely stating that you managed a successful project, share how working on that project made you realize the importance of team synergy and innovation. This emotional element creates a deeper connection and makes your story more memorable.

Utilize your narrative to connect effectively with colleagues and clients. In the corporate world, relationships are built on trust, mutual respect, and shared experiences. Your narrative serves as a bridge in this regard, allowing others to see your journey, values, and vision. When colleagues understand your story, they're more likely to support your goals and collaborate effectively. For clients, a well-crafted narrative can provide insights into your professional identity and reassure them of your commitment and competence.

The delivery of your narrative also matters. Whether it's a formal presentation, a casual conversation, or a written bio, the way you present your story should be engaging and consistent. Pay attention to your tone, body language, and the context in which you're sharing your narrative. Tailor your delivery to your audience, but ensure the core message remains intact.

Incorporating feedback is another crucial step in refining your narrative. Gather insights from trusted colleagues, mentors, or coaches who can provide perspectives on how your story is perceived. Honest feedback can help you identify any gaps or inconsistencies in your narrative, allowing you to make necessary adjustments and present a more polished and cohesive story.

Moreover, enhance your narrative by integrating it into your personal brand across various platforms. Your LinkedIn profile, professional website, and even social media channels should consistently reflect the key elements of your narrative. This cohesiveness ensures that whether someone meets you in person, reads about you online, or hears about you from others, they receive a consistent and compelling message about who you are and what you stand for.

Finally, remember that your personal narrative is not set in stone. As you grow and evolve in your career, so will your story. Regularly revisit and revise your narrative to reflect new experiences, insights, and goals. This ongoing refinement ensures that your personal brand remains relevant and resonant with your professional journey and aspirations.

In conclusion, creating a compelling personal narrative involves reflecting on pivotal moments, aligning them with your professional goals, crafting an emotionally engaging story, and consistently communicating it across various platforms. By doing so, you'll not only build a strong personal brand but also forge deeper connections with those around you, guiding and enriching your career path in the corporate world.

Enhancing Your Online Presence

In today's interconnected world, enhancing your online presence isn't just an option; it's a necessity for anyone looking to thrive as a corporate executive. With the digital realm being a primary avenue for showcasing your skills and expertise, it's imperative to present yourself strategically.

Let's begin with professional profiles, particularly LinkedIn. Your LinkedIn profile often serves as your digital handshake. It's the first impression you make before you even walk into an interview room or attend a professional meeting. Every element on your profile, from your headshot to your job descriptions, should be meticulously curated.

Your headshot should be professional yet approachable. Avoid using casual snapshots; instead, opt for a professionally taken photograph that exudes confidence and accessibility. Don't overlook the headline either. This small snippet carries weight. Aim to use a compelling title that not only states your current position but also highlights your expertise and aspirations. Think of it as a billboard that advertises your skills succinctly.

Next, your summary section. This is your chance to tell your story in a captivating and articulate manner. Harness this space to share your journey, your achievements, and your aspirations. Paint a picture of who you are as a professional but don't shy away from injecting a bit of personality. People connect with people, not just job titles. Use actionable language, highlight key milestones, and remember to infuse a narrative that captures your unique value proposition.

The experiences and roles listed should be more than just mundane job descriptions. Each entry should demonstrate impact. Use bullet points to outline your key responsibilities, but more importantly, emphasize results. Quantify your achievements where possible. Instead of saying you 'managed a team,' say you 'led a team of 10 professionals to achieve a 30% increase in quarterly sales.' It's details like these that make your profile stand out.

From ordinary to extraordinary

But LinkedIn is just one part of the puzzle. While it remains a critical platform, don't discount the value of optimizing your presence on other relevant platforms. Depending on your industry, websites like GitHub, Dribbble, or even specialized forums can be invaluable. Tailor your profiles on these sites much like you would on LinkedIn, but with a focus on the particular industry standards and expectations.

Creating a personal website or blog can be another powerful tool to showcase your expertise. Consider this your digital home, a space entirely under your control. It allows you to present a cohesive personal brand unhindered by the format constraints of social media platforms.

Start with a clean, professional design. The user experience should be your top priority; ensure that your website is easy to navigate and visually appealing. Use high-quality images and a consistent color scheme that aligns with your personal brand. Your website should include a comprehensive 'About Me' section that delves deeper into your professional journey. Highlight your unique skills, key accomplishments, and include anecdotes that provide a fuller picture of who you are.

Don't forget to showcase your expertise through a portfolio of your work. Whether it's projects you've managed, articles you've written, or presentations you've delivered, this section serves as tangible proof of your capabilities. Coupled with this, a regularly updated blog can further establish you as an authority in your field. Share insights, discuss industry trends, and offer valuable advice. This not only demonstrates your knowledge but also your commitment to continual learning and thought leadership.

Your online presence extends beyond your profiles and personal website. It's also shaped by your interactions and how you engage with your professional community. On platforms like LinkedIn, be an active participant. Share interesting articles, comment on discussions, and participate in relevant groups. Your contributions can significantly enhance your visibility and credibility.

Consider hosting webinars or live sessions where you can share your expertise more directly. These interactive formats not only position you as a sector specialist but also provide an opportunity for real-time engagement with your audience. It's a fantastic way to build a network of professionals who respect and value your insights.

Engagement also comes from what you endorse and support. Be mindful of the causes and content you align with publicly. Curating your digital endorsements to reflect your professional values and interests matters. This aspect of your online presence can sometimes speak louder than the content you create yourself.

It's equally important to manage your digital footprint. Regularly search your name online to see what appears. Adjust privacy settings on personal social media profiles and be proactive about controlling what's accessible to the public. The goal is to ensure that when someone searches for you, they find a professional, cohesive representation of who you are.

Enhancing your online presence is an ongoing task. It requires diligence, consistency, and a strategic approach. However, the effort invested here can pay massive dividends. As you continue to refine and expand your digital footprint, you propagate a personal brand that resonates with authenticity, expertise, and leadership. This, in turn, opens doors, creating opportunities for career growth and professional excellence.

Leveraging Public Speaking and Writing

Crafting your personal brand is a multifaceted endeavor, blending elements of self-awareness, strategic communication, and consistent effort. A powerful way to elevate and solidify your brand is through public speaking and writing. Whether you're addressing an audience at

From ordinary to extraordinary

a high-profile conference or writing an insightful article for a well-respected industry publication, these platforms offer unparalleled opportunities to showcase your expertise, establish authority, and create a memorable impression.

Public speaking is more than just delivering a polished speech. It's an opportunity to connect with your audience on a deeper level, sharing not only your knowledge but also your passion and vision. Look for speaking opportunities at conferences, workshops, and industry events. Participating in these will allow you to share your insights, demonstrate thought leadership, and engage directly with peers and leaders in your field. Preparation is crucial; rehearse your presentations thoroughly and be ready to handle questions with confidence and humility.

The impact of public speaking extends beyond the immediate audience. Recorded talks or live-streamed sessions can reach a global audience, amplifying your message and influence far and wide. Embrace this broader reach by ensuring that your speaking engagements are recorded and shared across multiple platforms. This not only maximizes your visibility but also serves as valuable content you can repurpose for other purposes, such as creating video snippets for social media or embedding in blog posts.

Writing is another key avenue for branding yourself as an authority. Authoring articles for industry publications, corporate blogs, or even LinkedIn provides you with a stage to express your perspectives and share your knowledge. Written content adds depth to your brand, allowing for nuanced arguments and thoughtful insights that might be difficult to convey in fleeting moments of conversation. Start by identifying the themes and topics that resonate with your target audience. Do they need help with emerging industry trends, or are they seeking advice on overcoming common challenges? Addressing these points can position you as a valuable source of information.

Your writing should be engaging and clear. Avoid jargon and overly complex sentences that could alienate readers. Instead, write in a way that is accessible and relatable, using anecdotes and examples to bring your points to life. This not only helps readers connect with your message but also makes your content more memorable. Consistency is key here; maintaining a regular writing schedule, whether it's bi-weekly articles or monthly contributions, helps keep your brand on the audience's radar.

Collaborations can also bolster your brand. Co-author articles with other experts, or contribute to respected industry blogs and newsletters. These partnerships can introduce you to new audiences and enhance your credibility through association. Networking with editors and influencers in your field can open doors to more prestigious writing opportunities and even potential speaking engagements.

When you combine speaking and writing, the synergy amplifies your brand exponentially. The feedback and experiences gained from public speaking can inform the topics you choose to write about, making your written content even more relevant and impactful. Conversely, the research and reflection involved in writing can enrich your speaking engagements, equipping you with a deeper well of knowledge to draw from.

Balancing these activities with your primary corporate responsibilities requires effective time management. Prioritize speaking and writing opportunities that align closely with your professional goals and personal interests. This ensures that your efforts not only build your brand but also contribute meaningfully to your career trajectory.

Maintaining a digital portfolio of your speaking and writing work is crucial. Create a section on your professional website or LinkedIn profile where visitors can easily access your talks, articles, and other relevant content. This serves as a living resume, showcasing your expertise and thought leadership to anyone who wishes to learn more about you.

Finally, remember that both public speaking and writing are skills that improve with practice. Seek feedback from trusted colleagues and mentors, and be open to constructive criticism. Attend workshops or take courses to refine your skills and stay updated on best practices. Over time, as your proficiency and confidence grow, so too will the strength and influence of your personal brand.

Leveraging these tools effectively can set you apart in the corporate world, demonstrating not just what you know, but also your ability to inspire, educate, and lead.

Chapter 9: Taking Action

You've laid the groundwork with knowledge and preparation; now it's time to take decisive action. In this chapter, we delve into the real-world application of the principles you've mastered so far. Action isn't just about grand gestures; it's the accumulation of deliberate, thoughtful steps that propel you toward your goals. We will explore compelling case studies and real-world examples of corporate leaders who epitomize the art of taking action. Alongside these, actionable tips and exercises will be provided to help you integrate these strategies into your daily life. Expert interviews will offer deeper insights, enriching your understanding of what it takes to bridge the gap between planning and execution. Remember, success in the corporate world doesn't come to those who wait but to those who seize the opportunity and act with purpose.

Case Studies and Examples

Imagine you are an executive at a bustling global company, where the demands of the job often stretch beyond the traditional workday. The path to maintaining peak performance and mental clarity in such a high-pressure environment calls for more than just natural talent—it requires the mindset of a "corporate athlete." In this section, we'll explore real-life examples of individuals who have harnessed physical, mental, and emotional conditioning to thrive in the corporate world.

Meet Jane Thompson, the CEO of a leading technology firm. Jane's journey is a prime example of how physical fitness can fuel professional success. She realized early in her career that her daily energy levels and capacity for handling stress were directly linked to her physical health. Jane committed to a rigorous exercise routine that included morning runs and evening yoga sessions. Her disciplined approach to physical fitness not only enhanced her stamina but also improved her mental resilience. By maintaining a balanced lifestyle, Jane has consistently led her company to new heights, surviving recessions and spearheading successful product launches.

Another exemplary corporate athlete is Steve Marshall, a renowned financial advisor. Stress management became his forte after he significantly revamped his daily habits. Initially, Steve found himself frequently overwhelmed by the fast-paced nature of financial markets. He decided to undergo mindfulness training, incorporating meditation and deep-breathing exercises into his daily regimen. These practices transformed his ability to focus during critical trading hours and, in turn, increased his client satisfaction ratings and success rate in making profitable trades. Steve's story demonstrates how mental conditioning can enable professionals to perform at their peak, even under intense pressure.

Consider the case of Maria Rodriguez, the CMO of a multinational consumer goods company. For Maria, emotional intelligence played a crucial role in her climb up the corporate ladder. She invested time in understanding her own emotional triggers and developed strategies to manage them effectively. Maria also prioritized building genuine relationships with her colleagues and subordinates. She practiced active listening and provided constructive feedback, which fostered a positive and collaborative work environment. Her emotional acumen allowed her to lead a high-performance marketing team that consistently outperformed its targets, earning her recognition and promotions.

A holistic approach to maintaining peak performance in the corporate arena was epitomized by the late Phil Knight, co-founder of Nike. Phil's story is a remarkable case of balancing physical, mental, and emotional well-being. Despite managing a rapidly growing global brand, Phil remained an avid runner. His passion for running not only inspired Nike's product line but also kept him grounded. Phil's ability to stay physically active while simultaneously driving forward a company culture rooted in innovation and perseverance made him a quintessential corporate athlete.

Another fascinating example is Elon Musk, the CEO of multiple pioneering companies like Tesla and SpaceX. Elon's approach to time management and productivity is legendary. He meticulously plans his day in five-minute slots and prioritizes tasks with an ironclad focus. This disciplined approach enables him to juggle the responsibilities of multiple high-stakes roles without compromising on creativity or output. Elon's story emphasizes the importance of strategic time management as a core component of corporate athleticism.

Let's examine Sarah Nguyen, Head of HR at a multinational conglomerate. Sarah stands out for her commitment to continuous learning and adaptability. She regularly participates in industry conferences, attends advanced HR workshops, and pursues online certifications. This continual upskilling ensures she stays ahead of the curve in an ever-evolving field. By fostering a culture of learning within her team, Sarah has been able to implement innovative HR practices that have significantly improved employee satisfaction and retention rates.

Another notable example is Tim Cook, CEO of Apple. Known for his early morning workouts and regimented schedule, Tim embodies the principles of physical conditioning for optimal performance. He begins his day with a workout at 5 a.m., which sets a disciplined tone for the rest of the day. Tim's routine is a testament to how physical fitness can enhance productivity and mental sharpness, crucial for steering one of the world's most influential companies.

These case studies underscore the fact that thriving in the corporate world requires more than expertise in one's professional domain. It demands a balanced approach to physical, mental, and emotional well-being. The individuals profiled here have not merely adapted to the high demands of their roles; they have excelled by conditioning themselves as corporate athletes, proving that success is a holistic endeavor.

The narrative of each corporate athlete is unique, yet common threads bind them. Discipline, resilience, adaptability, and a commitment to continuous improvement are paramount. Their journeys are inspirational and serve as roadmaps for others aiming to achieve similar heights in their careers.

As we continue, we'll delve deeper into actionable tips and exercises you can incorporate into your own routine, along with insights from industry experts who have mastered the art of being a corporate athlete. These strategies, combined with the inspirational stories shared here, will equip you to take actionable steps towards excelling in the demanding world of corporate leadership.

Actionable Tips and Exercises

Transitioning from theory to practice can be daunting, but it's a crucial step on your journey to becoming a successful corporate executive. Below, you'll find a series of practical exercises and tips that you can implement immediately. These actionable steps are designed to help you condition your mind and body, enhance your emotional intelligence, and develop leadership skills, thus preparing you to take action with confidence.

1. Daily Physical Fitness Routine

A well-rounded fitness regimen is essential for maintaining optimal performance. Start with a manageable routine and gradually increase the intensity. Here's a sample to get you going:

- **Warm-Up:** Spend 5–10 minutes on light cardio, such as jogging or jumping jacks.
- **Strength Training:** Perform 3 sets of 10–12 reps of basic exercises like push-ups, squats, and lunges.
- **Cardio:** Incorporate 20–30 minutes of sustained cardio activity, such as running, cycling, or swimming.
- **Cool Down:** Finish with 5–10 minutes of stretching to relax your muscles.

Tip: Use an app to track your progress and stay motivated. Setting realistic goals and monitoring your achievements can provide a sense of accomplishment and keep you committed.

2. Mental Toughness Drills

Mental conditioning is just as vital as physical fitness. To build mental toughness and resilience, try the following exercises:

- **Mindfulness Meditation:** Spend 10 minutes each morning practicing mindfulness. Focus on your breath, and let go of any distractions.
- **Positive Visualization:** Visualize yourself achieving your goals. Imagine the steps you'll take and the obstacles you'll overcome. Doing this can significantly boost your confidence.
- **Gratitude Journal:** Write down three things you're grateful for each day. This can shift your focus from stressors to positive aspects of your life.

Exercise: Commit to a 30-day mental toughness challenge. Each day, select an exercise from above and record how it impacts your mindset. Reflect on your progress and adjust as needed.

3. Emotional Intelligence Enhancements

Understanding and managing your emotions are foundational skills for effective leadership. Here are some practical ways to enhance your emotional intelligence:

- **Active Listening:** Practice active listening by paying full attention to the speaker and providing feedback to show that you understand their message.
- **Empathy Exercises:** Try to see situations from others' perspectives. Ask yourself how you would feel if you were in their shoes.
- **Self-Reflection:** Spend a few minutes at the end of each day reflecting on your interactions. Identify what went well and what could be improved.

Exercise: Conduct an "emotional audit" of your daily interactions. Note instances where you handled situations well and areas where you can improve. Aim to enhance at least one interpersonal skill each week.

4. Time Management Techniques

Time management is a critical skill for executives. Enhance your productivity with these techniques:

- **Prioritization Matrix:** Use the Eisenhower Box to categorize tasks by urgency and importance. Focus on tasks that are important but not urgent to prevent last-minute stress.
- **Time Blocking:** Allocate specific time blocks for different tasks. This helps prevent multitasking and allows for deep work on high-priority items.

- **Pomodoro Technique:** Work in 25-minute intervals (Pomodoros) followed by a 5-minute break. After four Pomodoros, take a longer break of 15–30 minutes.

Exercise: Create a weekly schedule using the time blocking method. At the end of the week, review your progress and adjust your approach based on what worked and what didn't.

5. Leadership Skill Development

Effective leadership requires continuous development. Use these tips to sharpen your skills:

- **Seek Feedback:** Regularly ask colleagues for feedback on your leadership style and areas for improvement.
- **Mentorship:** Engage with a mentor who can provide guidance and share their experiences. Additionally, mentor others to reinforce your own learning.
- **Leadership Courses:** Enroll in leadership development programs or courses. These can provide new perspectives and practical strategies.

Tip: Practice situational leadership. Adapt your leadership style based on the needs of your team and the task at hand. This flexibility can result in better team dynamics and effectiveness.

6. Continuous Learning and Adaptability

The corporate world is ever-evolving, and staying adaptable is crucial. Here are some strategies to keep learning and remain agile:

- **Reading Habit:** Dedicate time daily or weekly to read industry reports, books, and articles to stay updated on trends and innovations.

- **Webinars and Workshops:** Attend webinars and workshops related to your field. These can offer both knowledge and networking opportunities.
- **Experimentation:** Don't be afraid to try new approaches in your work. Innovation often comes from taking calculated risks.

Exercise: Set a quarterly learning goal. This could be completing a course, attending a certain number of webinars, or reading specific books. Track your progress and reflect on how it impacts your professional growth.

7. Personal Branding Activities

Your personal brand is a reflection of your reputation and unique value. Building and maintaining it requires deliberate effort:

- **Identify Your Strengths:** List your strengths and areas where you can truly add value. Craft a personal narrative around these attributes.
- **Online Presence:** Update your LinkedIn profile and ensure it aligns with your personal brand. Regularly share content that showcases your expertise.
- **Public Speaking:** Participate in speaking engagements to increase your visibility. Toastmasters or similar groups can provide platforms to hone this skill.

Exercise: Develop a 30-second elevator pitch. Practice delivering it until you can confidently articulate your unique value proposition in any professional setting.

8. Creating a Personal Action Plan

Finally, tie all these activities together

Interviews and Expert Insights:

As we delved into what it takes to become a successful corporate executive, it became apparent that insights from seasoned professionals could provide unparalleled value. This section captures anecdotes and wisdom shared by corporate athletes, industry leaders, and field experts, offering a multifaceted perspective on implementing strategies for success.

When we sat down with Jessica Thompson, CEO of a leading tech firm, she highlighted the non-negotiables of maintaining physical health. "The cornerstone of my daily routine is a one-hour workout," she explained. "It's not just about staying fit, but it helps me clear my mind and prepare for the mental rigors of the day. This practice has been pivotal in my career, right from my early days as a junior analyst to my current role here."

But Jessica isn't alone in this belief. Paul Donovan, a renowned leadership coach, emphasized the crucial job that physical conditioning holds in building mental resilience. "Physical fitness and mental toughness go hand in hand," Paul noted. "When an executive dedicates time to physical exercise, they inadvertently train themselves for better discipline, endurance, and performance under stress."

Diving into the realm of mental conditioning, Dr. Elaine Murphy, a cognitive psychologist who collaborates with top executives, shared valuable insights. "Building mental toughness isn't just about enduring long hours," she said. "It involves nurturing a mindset that welcomes challenges and views failures as learning opportunities." Murphy emphasized the significance of mindfulness practices and daily gratitude exercises to build a resilient mind.

Dr. Murphy's words were echoed by John Richards, a highly regarded financial strategist. "In my line of work, the ability to stay composed under pressure can make or break deals," John pointed out. "I can't stress enough the value of stress management techniques. The time I spend on developing a clear, focused mind through meditation has significantly reduced my stress levels and increased my decision-making accuracy."

The dialogue around emotional intelligence brought up fascinating viewpoints. Maria Lopez, Chief HR Officer of a multinational conglomerate, shared her experiences in navigating the complexities of corporate relationships. "Understanding and managing emotions is pivotal for building and sustaining strong team dynamics," she remarked. "I've implemented emotional intelligence workshops that not only boost morale but also improve overall team performance."

Kate Hannigan, a renowned business consultant, agreed and went further to discuss the role of empathy in leadership. "Leaders who can genuinely connect with their teams foster an environment of trust and collaboration," she shared. "This is not just about being 'nice'. Empathy helps in understanding motivation and aligning individual goals with organizational objectives."

From the perspective of time management and productivity, insights came from Michael Lee, an entrepreneur known for his efficiency. "Mastering time management was a game-changer for me," Michael emphasized. "Prioritizing tasks and setting SMART goals enable you to focus on what truly matters without spreading yourself too thin. The real trick is to schedule downtime as rigorously as you schedule meetings."

In our conversation with Susan Patel, a highly effective project manager at a Fortune 500 company, she expounded on techniques that maximize efficiency. "I'm a big advocate for the Pomodoro Technique and using project management software," Susan shared. "These tools have not only streamlined my workflow but also made it easier for me to visualize progress and adjust strategies in real-time."

The narrative around leadership and team dynamics unearthed powerful truths. David Collins, who heads one of the most profitable divisions at a major conglomerate, shared his mantra: "A leader's primary job is to create other leaders," he stated. "Investing in team development and taking a genuine interest in their personal and professional growth pays off in unimaginable ways."

Laura Bennett, an executive at a global manufacturing giant, revealed her secret to building high-performance teams: "Transparency and accountability. When team members are clear about their roles and responsibilities and have a transparent view of the project goals, they perform better." Laura added, "I often use team-building exercises that focus on real-life projects. It helps in practical skill development and strengthens team cohesion."

Moreover, continuous learning and adaptability emerged as critical themes during our discussions. Jennifer Yang, a noted advocate for lifelong learning, elaborated on its importance. "The corporate landscape is ever-changing. If you're not evolving, you're falling behind," she warned. "I allocate time each week for either taking online courses or attending industry seminars.

Adding to this, Sam Stevenson, a C-level executive well-versed in change management, shared his approach: "Flexibility is key," Sam advised. "Being open to new ideas and adaptable to changing business environments sets the foundation for sustainable success. This can't be overstated."

Emily Turner, a self-made thought leader in the tech industry, provided candid thoughts on crafting a personal brand. "Your brand is your professional footprint. People remember you not just for your skills but also for your values and how you carry yourself," Emily emphasized. "I've consistently worked on aligning my personal values with my professional goals to create a compelling narrative."

Echoing Emily's sentiments, Sarah O'Neil, an acclaimed public speaker and author, shared her strategy: "Gaining feedback is crucial," Sarah asserted. "Understanding how others perceive you allows you to adjust and refine your personal brand. It's a continuous endeavor that requires both introspection and external input."

These valued insights and narratives from industry trailblazers and experts not only elucidate the strategies for achieving excellence in the corporate world but also offer readers actionable takeaways. From the non-negotiable pillar of physical fitness to the fine art of time management, from leadership dynamics to personal branding, the paths to corporate success are varied and nuanced. What remains constant, though, is the unwavering commitment to personal and professional growth. By weaving these practices into your life, you can not only aim for but achieve the lofty heights of corporate achievement.

Conclusion

As we reach the culmination of our journey through the intricacies of becoming a successful corporate executive, it is time to reflect on the profound transformations that await those who diligently apply the principles discussed. The road to success in the corporate world is neither short nor straight, but it is one that rewards perseverance, strategic thinking, and continuous improvement.

At the core of this transformation lies the concept of the corporate athlete. Similar to professional athletes, corporate leaders must strive for an optimal balance of physical, mental, and emotional conditioning. The essence of this balance is not just in achieving professional success but also in sustaining it over the long term.

Physical fitness forms the foundation on which the corporate athlete builds their career. It is the bedrock that offers resilience against stress, enhances cognitive functions, and promotes overall well-being. A disciplined exercise routine, much like the ones professional athletes adhere to, can significantly boost an executive's energy levels and performance.

Yet, physical prowess must be complemented by mental toughness. In the corporate arena, mental conditioning is about far more than just intelligence. It's about resilience against challenges, the capability to stay focused under pressure, and the ability to cultivate a mindset that views obstacles as opportunities for growth. By incorporating effective stress management techniques and fostering mental agility, one can navigate the corporate landscape with a clear vision and steadfast resolve.

Equally crucial is the realm of emotional intelligence. Understanding and managing one's emotions, while effectively interpreting and responding to the emotions of others, forms the bedrock of strong interpersonal relationships and effective communication. These skills are indispensable for leaders who aim to inspire and motivate their teams, creating a harmonious and productive work environment.

Time management and productivity are pillars holding up the structure of a successful corporate career. Prioritizing tasks, setting clear goals, and adopting methods to maximize efficiency not only enhance individual performance but also contribute to the overall success of the organization. Time is a finite resource; thus, those who master its management invariably find themselves a step ahead.

Leadership is often seen as the pinnacle of executive qualities. Effective leaders are not just knowledgeable and skilled; they are also visionaries who can inspire others to achieve greatness. Building high-performance teams, setting a clear direction, and fostering a culture of trust and innovation are the hallmarks of exceptional leadership.

In an ever-evolving corporate world, the ability to learn continuously and adapt to change cannot be overstated. Lifelong learning keeps executives abreast of the latest trends, skills, and technologies, making them more adaptable to changes and better equipped to lead their organizations through transformation.

Reflecting on these principles, it becomes evident that the journey toward becoming a successful corporate executive is a holistic one. It is a continuous process of self-improvement and adaptation, grounded in a balanced approach to physical, mental, and emotional well-being.

To truly excel, one must embrace the mindset of a lifelong learner and a resilient leader. This journey is not just about the destination; it's about the ongoing process of growth and improvement. By following the guidance provided in this book, you are not merely preparing for success in the corporate world; you are setting the stage for a lifetime of achievement and fulfillment.

In conclusion, the path to becoming a successful corporate executive is paved with challenges that test one's endurance, intellect, and emotional fortitude. It requires a multifaceted approach that combines physical fitness, mental resilience, emotional intelligence, effective time management, and continuous learning. By embracing these principles and committing to ongoing self-improvement, you are equipped to face the corporate world with confidence and grace. The journey is continuous, the rewards immense, and the impact on your life and those around you, profound.

As you venture forth, remember that the essence of true success lies not just in reaching the pinnacle of your career, but in the wisdom, balance, and strength you cultivate along the way. May you navigate your corporate journey with unwavering resolve and an enduring commitment to excellence.

Appendix A: Appendix

The journey toward becoming a successful corporate executive is a multifaceted endeavor. This appendix serves as an added layer of support, offering a collection of resources and recommended readings that can supplement the material covered throughout this book. Below, you'll find sections dedicated to tools, methodologies, and literature that provide further insights into the physical, mental, and emotional conditioning required to excel in the corporate sphere.

Additional Resources

It's essential to have access to reliable resources that can help bolster your understanding and implementation of the concepts discussed in the previous chapters. The following resources have been curated to provide practical tools and strategies:

- **Physical Conditioning Tools:** Explore apps and online platforms that offer custom workout plans tailored to busy professionals. Look for features that include flexibility, cardiovascular, and strength training exercises that can be performed with minimal equipment.

- **Mental Conditioning Resources:** Consider subscribing to meditation and mindfulness apps that can help you develop mental toughness. These platforms often include guided sessions, breathing exercises, and cognitive behavioral techniques designed for peak mental performance.

- **Emotional Intelligence Assessment Tools:** Utilize online assessments to gauge your emotional intelligence. These tools can provide valuable feedback on your emotional awareness, management skills, and relationship-building capabilities.
- **Time Management Software:** Implement productivity tools and apps that focus on goal setting, task prioritization, and efficiency tracking. Look for features that integrate seamlessly into your daily workflow.
- **Leadership Development Programs:** Enroll in workshops and online courses that focus on developing leadership skills and understanding team dynamics. Programs accredited by reputable institutions often provide the most up-to-date information and best practices.

Recommended Readings

The following books are highly recommended for further exploration of themes related to physical, mental, and emotional growth within the corporate world. These readings offer a deep dive into various aspects of professional development and provide actionable insights:

1. "The Corporate Athlete" by Jack L. Groppel - A comprehensive guide on optimizing work performance through physical fitness and mental resilience.
2. "Emotional Intelligence 2.0" by Travis Bradberry and Jean Greaves - A practical approach to developing your emotional intelligence skills in a professional setting.
3. "Atomic Habits" by James Clear - This book outlines the power of small habits and incremental changes in achieving long-term goals.

4. "Deep Work" by Cal Newport - A manifesto on the importance of focused work in achieving significant professional accomplishments.
5. "The 7 Habits of Highly Effective People" by Stephen R. Covey - An enduring classic that covers essential principles for personal and professional effectiveness.
6. "Leaders Eat Last" by Simon Sinek - An exploration of the qualities that make great leaders and how to build high-performing teams.

In conclusion, the additional resources and recommended readings provided in this appendix are intended to enhance your journey towards becoming a formidable corporate executive. By leveraging these tools and delving into these insightful books, you'll be well-equipped to navigate the complexities of the corporate world with confidence and poise.

Additional Resources

In the journey towards becoming a successful corporate executive, the path can be unpredictable and challenging. However, equipping oneself with the right tools and knowledge can significantly ease this journey. Beyond the chapters of this book, there are numerous resources that can further aid in your development. These additional resources encompass various forms of media, including books, articles, podcasts, and online courses that can offer further insights and expand your understanding of the principles discussed in this book.

Firstly, consider exploring books that delve deeper into concepts of leadership, emotional intelligence, and time management. Texts like "Emotional Intelligence" by Daniel Goleman and "Leaders Eat Last" by Simon Sinek offer profound insights into leadership and personal development. These books provide case studies, real-world examples, and practical techniques which can be incredibly beneficial.

In addition to these, academic journals and articles from reputable sources like Harvard Business Review and Forbes often publish pieces on emerging trends and strategies in corporate management. Subscribing to these can keep you updated on the latest research and industry practices, ensuring that your knowledge remains current and relevant.

Podcasts are another excellent resource for continuous learning. Programs such as "The Tim Ferriss Show" or "The Tony Robbins Podcast" feature interviews with business leaders, entrepreneurs, and thought leaders who share their experiences and insights. Listening to these podcasts during your commute or workout can be an efficient way to gain knowledge and inspiration.

For those who prefer interactive learning, online courses from platforms like Coursera, edX, and LinkedIn Learning can be highly beneficial. These courses cover a wide range of topics relevant to corporate success, from strategic management to mental resilience. Many of these platforms offer certificates upon completion, which can be added to your professional portfolio.

Another vital resource is mentorship. Finding a mentor within your industry can provide personalized guidance and feedback that books and courses might lack. Mentors can share their experiences, provide networking opportunities, and help you navigate the unique challenges of your career.

Networking events and professional groups can also be valuable. Joining organizations like the Young Presidents' Organization (YPO) or attending industry conferences can provide opportunities to connect with peers and leaders in your field, fostering a network of support and collaboration.

Don't underestimate the power of community. Online forums and discussion groups, such as those on Reddit or LinkedIn, can be excellent spaces to ask questions, share experiences, and gain insights from a diverse group of professionals.

Effective use of technology can also streamline your path to corporate success. Tools and apps that aid in time management, project management, and communication—like Asana, Trello, or Slack—can improve productivity and efficiency, allowing you to focus on strategic tasks and leadership responsibilities.

Consider engaging in workshops and seminars, both online and in person. These often provide hands-on learning experiences and can cover specialized topics in greater depth than broader resources. Many workshops also offer opportunities for one-on-one coaching and immediate feedback.

Lastly, do not underestimate the wealth of information available through public resources like libraries and educational websites. Many library systems offer access to business journals, eBooks, and even free online courses. Websites like Khan Academy and MIT OpenCourseWare provide free lessons on a wide range of topics, providing additional avenues for self-improvement.

By leveraging these additional resources, you can continue to build on the foundation provided in this book. Remember, the journey to becoming a successful corporate executive never truly ends; it is a continuous process of learning, adapting, and growing. With a commitment to professional development and a proactive approach to utilizing available resources, you can navigate the corporate world with confidence and resilience.

Recommended Readings

As you endeavor to excel in the corporate world, it will be paramount to engage in continuous learning and gather varied perspectives. The recommended readings in this section have been carefully curated to complement the themes discussed throughout the book and to provide additional insights that are critical for a successful corporate executive.

One crucial book to consider is **"The Power of Habit"** by Charles Duhigg. This book delves into the science of habits and how they can be transformed for personal and professional success. Duhigg's narrative makes complex scientific principles accessible, promoting a deep understanding of how habits are formed and how they can be changed. For a corporate athlete, mastering habits can be transformative for physical conditioning, productivity, and leadership potential.

"Emotional Intelligence 2.0" by Travis Bradberry and Jean Greaves is another indispensable read. Emotional intelligence, as we've discussed, is vital for building strong relationships and effective communication. This book provides practical advice and strategies to enhance your emotional intelligence, backed by research and real-world examples. It's a step-by-step guide that can immediately impact your work environment.

In the realm of mental conditioning and resilience, **"Grit: The Power of Passion and Perseverance"** by Angela Duckworth stands out. Duckworth explores the role of grit—a combination of passion and perseverance—in achieving high levels of success. This book can offer immense value for those seeking to build mental toughness, an essential trait in leading teams and handling corporate challenges.

Leadership literature offers vast resources, but John C. Maxwell's **"The 21 Irrefutable Laws of Leadership"** remains a cornerstone. Maxwell outlines time-tested principles that are universal to leadership effectiveness. Whether you're aiming to lead a high-performance team or enhance your own leadership capabilities, this book offers practical and actionable insights.

For mastering time management and productivity, David Allen's **"Getting Things Done: The Art of Stress-Free Productivity"** is a must-read. Allen provides a detailed system for organizing tasks and priorities to ensure maximum efficiency without the burnout. His methodology has helped many executives transform their productivity practices, making it an invaluable resource for incorporating the principles of efficient task management discussed in Chapter 5.

Change is often the only constant in the corporate world, and adaptability is a crucial skill. **"Who Moved My Cheese?"** by Spencer Johnson is a timeless parable about managing change. While seemingly simple, its lessons are profound and relevant to anyone facing shifts in their corporate environment. It's an easy read with lasting impact, reinforcing the importance of adaptability as highlighted in Chapter 7.

Another essential read for corporate athletes is **"Atomic Habits: An Easy & Proven Way to Build Good Habits & Break Bad Ones"** by James Clear. Building on the foundation laid by Duhigg, Clear's book deconstructs the process of habit formation into manageable steps and offers a clear roadmap for integrating effective habits into your daily routine. This can be a powerful tool for both personal and professional development.

The landscape of emotional intelligence can be further examined through Daniel Goleman's **"Emotional Intelligence: Why It Can Matter More Than IQ"**. Goleman's work remains seminal in understanding the broad applications of emotional intelligence in various spheres of life, including the corporate domain. It will provide deeper insights into the discussions highlighted in Chapter 4.

Besides books, articles, journals, and research papers serve as excellent complementary resources. Harvard Business Review, for instance, publishes numerous articles on leadership, productivity, and organizational behavior. Regular engagement with such materials can keep you updated with the latest trends and scholarly research in the corporate world.

Adopting a holistic learning approach is also beneficial. Online platforms like Coursera, edX, and LinkedIn Learning offer courses on leadership, emotional intelligence, time management, and other relevant subjects. These courses often feature content from leading universities and professionals in the field, offering a structured learning path.

Joining professional book clubs or discussion groups can also enhance your understanding of these materials. Engaging in discussions about key concepts and real-world applications can deepen your comprehension and allow you to see different perspectives. Networking with like-minded professionals who are also on a journey of continuous improvement can provide additional support and motivation.

In conclusion, as you navigate your path to becoming a successful corporate executive, the recommended readings listed here serve as vital tools. They will not only reinforce the concepts discussed in this book but also broaden your knowledge and skills. Remember, the journey to excellence is ongoing and multifaceted. These resources provide an invaluable toolkit to help you condition your mind, body, and spirit for the corporate arena.

Building a library of such impactful reading materials and revisiting them regularly will be an investment in your growth. These books and resources are more than just words on a page—they entrench essential principles and methodologies that can propel your career forward. Combine these readings with the insights and practices discussed throughout this book, and you'll be well on your way to achieving unparalleled success in the corporate world.

Made in United States
Orlando, FL
06 August 2024